"Passing" For Who You Really Are

Essays in Support of Multiracial Whiteness

A.D. Powell

Backintyme
Palm Coast, Florida, U.S.A.

Backintyme
30 Medford Drive
Palm Coast FL 32137-2504

386-446-4909
website: http://backintyme.com
email: sales@backintyme.com

Printed in the United States of America
First Printing, March 2005

ISBN: 0-939479-22-2

Library of Congress Control Number: 2005922055

In Memory of Anatole Broyard

A White/Caucasian/European American
of Multiracial Ancestry

Contents

Foreword
by Frank W. Sweet

A.D. Powell reminds you of H.L. Mencken. Like the famous columnist, she somehow drives intellectual midgets into frenzies of outrage, and the spectacle amuses and entertains her fans. It is not that what she writes is in error, or that it does not reflect factual reality—much to the contrary. Like Mencken, she writes with crystalline precision and merciless accuracy. The problem is that, like Mencken, she writes of Things Best Left Unsaid in America. Mencken once wrote:

> I believe that no discovery of fact, however trivial, can be wholly useless to the race, and that no trumpeting of falsehood, however virtuous in intent, can be anything but vicious. The whole thing, after all, may be put very simply. I believe that it is better to tell the truth than to lie. I believe that it is better to be free than to be a slave. And I believe that it is better to know than be ignorant. – H.L. Mencken

Unlike Mencken, who usually targeted America's political idiocies, Powell aims her barbs at liberals—White and Black—who preach the one-drop rule. She is the nemesis of those who advocate the uniquely American notion that there is no such thing as a White person with a trace of African ancestry—that such a person is, at best, a "light-skinned Black." The U.S. one-drop rule degrades reason, ignores science, crushes tolerance, outlaws ethnic choice, and mocks the American Dream. And yet it is preached as dogma by Liberals and its enforcement is demanded by Black political leaders.

Sadly, were it not for Ms. Powell and those like her, millions of well-meaning Americans would believe that, when it comes to "racial identity," it is better to lie that to tell the truth. That it is better to be a slave to manipulation than to be free. And that it is better to be ignorant than to know.

The essays in this collection were previously published in *Interracial Voice*, an internet-based online magazine published by Charles Byrd. Mr. Byrd graciously gave his permission for their reprinting here. With one exception, the essays are presented in the order in which they were published.

The first essay, *White Racial Identity, Racial Mixture, and the One Drop Rule*, is actually the one most recently written. It was a scholarly paper delivered in June 2004 at an academic conference sponsored by the Melungeon Heritage Association. It leads the collection because it is the most complete and persuasive exposition of Ms. Powell's thesis (that Americans are sadly blind to the implications of their peculiar one-drop rule).

"White," "Mixed" or "Other"? Some Books and Articles Your Librarian Didn't Tell you About! is a historians' bibliography. It is an annotated list of monographs showing that the one-drop rule is of recent origin and was virtually unknown during slavery.

Five of the essays, A *Political Alliance Between ALL Multiracial/Multiethnic Individuals!?*, *A.D. Powell vs. Marc Eisen, Harold McDougall at 'Multiracial Identities & The 2000 Census" Panel*, *The Problem With Gregory Howard Williams*, and *National Public Radio Promotes the "One Drop" Myth* are polemics. That is, they advocate multiracialism against those who support the one-drop notion. Although all illustrate the debate, the exchange with Marc Eisen, editor of a Wisconsin news weekly, is particularly informative. Like many Americans, the man is sincerely incapable of grasping that his insistence that Anatole Broyard was "really Black," despite appearance, despite genetics, despite Broyard's own choice of ethnicity, is in any way reprehensible. His response of ad-hominem contempt towards Ms. Powell is one of the two most common reactions to her criticism of the one-drop rule. (The other is to accuse Ms. Powell of being "secretly a Negro" and thereby a traitor to the "Black race.")

The essay *White Folks: A True Story* follows *The Problem With Gregory Howard Williams* because it shows an alternative ethnic choice. Williams chose to switch from being White to being Black in late childhood. He publicly rationalized his choice of Black ethnicity in a lucrative book that tugs all of the politically correct heartstrings. *White Folks*, in contrast, tells the tale of someone who switched from the Black community to the White in order to adopt an ethnicity that matched her actual genetic makeup.

Finally, the four essays: *When Are Irish-Americans Not Good Enough to be Irish-American?*, *Pissing on the Graves of Heroes*, *Racial Mixture, "White" Identity, and the "Forgotten" (or Censored) Cause of the Civil War*, and *Are "White" Americans All "Passing as White"?* are historical reviews. The first two are responses to publications that co-opted the memories of famous people and fraudulently "outed" them as secretly Black when in fact they were no more "secretly Black" than tens of millions of other White Americans. The latter two are reviews of recent historical monographs: one justifiably lauded by academia, the other unjustifiably ignored.

Enjoy.

I. White Racial Identity, Racial Mixture, and the One Drop Rule
Presented at Fifth Union, Kingsport, Tennessee
Friday, 18 June 2004

In the days of the Third Reich, the Nazis imposed the "Nuremberg Laws" on German citizens. Assimilated German Jews were told that they were not German. It didn't matter that their language, culture and self-image were all proudly German. They now belonged to a separate and "inferior race." Nazi propaganda pictured all Jews as racially distinct from Germans, but the reality was that Jews were forced to wear symbols of identification—yellow Stars of David—so they would not be able to "pass" as German or "Aryan." People with either one Jewish parent or grandparent found themselves reclassified as mischlings or "mixed race." The biographies of German Jews and part-Jews frequently speak of "passing for Aryan" and the desirability of having Nordic as opposed to darker or more Semitic looks because the former facilitated the ability to "pass." Are we having a feeling of deja vu yet?

While most Americans have been carefully taught that the Nazis were crazy, evil, racist, etc., for "seeing" separate "races" in Europe when they didn't exist, we are never asked to see the similarity between the Nuremberg Laws that defined Jews and mischlings and our own legal and social traditions of racial classification—especially the myth that white people with a "taint" of Jewish—excuse me—Negro blood are not truly white but secret, "light-skinned" members of the "black race" who are only "passing for white." Just as German Jews were declared unworthy of the honor of being German,

American laws, films, novels, television programs, etc., encourage Americans to accept the idea that even small amounts of "black blood" destroy all right to a European-American heritage and identity. The great difference is that, while the Nazis were avowed racists, today's American society is based on laws that enforce legal and social equality between the so-called "races." Indeed, the idea that otherwise white persons can be secret, hidden members of the black race, is promoted by many of the very people who pride themselves on fighting racism in others.

Documentary Genocide and "Lynching" Reputations

In its June 16, 1996 issue, the very liberal and prestigious *The New Yorker* magazine published an article by Harvard University Afro-American Studies professor Henry Louis Gates, Jr., in which he denounced the late, highly respected *New York Times* book critic and author, Anatole Broyard, as a "light-skinned black man" who had "passed for white." Entitled, "White Like Me: The True Lies of Anatole Broyard," Gates' article charged Broyard, who was of Louisiana Creole parentage, with "lying" about his "race" because he did not identify with blacks. The attack by Gates and *The New Yorker* was aimed not just at one man but at all Americans in a similar situation. It was an attack that Adolf Hitler and Walter Plecker would have enthusiastically supported.

Broyard had brought the blood of the "inferior" Negro race into the "superior" white race and "polluted" the latter. But wait! Our mainstream American media don't believe in superior and inferior races. In our society, the ideals of racial equality and opposition to racism are trumpeted from the rooftops. What's going on here?

A recent major motion picture, *The Human Stain* (and the novel that preceded it), also solemnly warned the nation that strange, inferior creatures it called "light-skinned blacks" had implanted themselves into the white race. Like the German Jews who looked German, acted German, etc., but were NOT truly German, these strange creatures looked and acted white but were most unworthy of that honor. It sounds almost like one of those horror movies in which aliens take over human bodies in an attempt to walk among us do us harm. Miramax, the company that produced the film, sent special instructions to movie critics to make sure that all of them knew about so-called "passing for white" and would describe the otherwise white protagonist, called "Coleman Silk," as a "light-skinned black man" who was guilty of the heinous crime of claiming the "honor" of being white when he was tainted by the blood of the inferior black race—excuse me, we don't believe in that anymore. He tainted the white race with the blood of the blacks in whose equality Miramax and all the other mainstream movie critics claim to believe.

Does this make sense? If a man tells you he's Irish and you later find out that he's also part-German, do you denounce him as a lying German who only "passed" for Irish? No, because Irish and Germans are considered biological and social equals. If our Irishman is part-German, you are not getting an inferior product. If our Irishman is part-Negro, he is no longer Irish because the Negro blood means you are getting an "inferior" person and not the "superior" person you thought he was. This makes sense if you're a racist who believes in white racial purity, but all these anti-passing accusations are made by people who claim to be against racism. Why is that?

The Human Stain was only the latest in a string of warnings about the white race being infiltrated by these alien, genetic freaks called "light-skinned blacks." While those Americans who lived through the pre-Civil Rights era, when racism (not anti-racism) was politically correct, are aware of the so-called "anti-miscegenation" laws that supposedly prevented Negro blood from entering the white race, most Americans probably learn this lesson from Hollywood. Constant television reruns of films such as the two versions of *Imitation of Life*, *Pinky* and various television programs present the horror movie scenario—the inferior, genetic freaks look like us but are not us.

American journalists who write about so-called "passing for white" solemnly inform the public that "one drop" of "black blood" makes you "black" in the United States of

America. They admit that this idea is rooted in the presumed inferiority of the race in whose equality they claim to believe. However, unlike other racist practices from the pre-Civil Rights era, we are told that the "one drop rule" is something we should embrace rather than scorn. We are told that those who reject the racism of the "one drop rule" are worthy of our contempt. Why the contradiction? Why is the "one drop" myth the only racist rule that self-described anti-racists in the media and academia are fighting to preserve? Why did the only credible and powerful opposition to the proposed "multiracial option" for the U.S. Census, for example, come from NAACP, the National Council of La Raza and other so-called civil rights organizations? Why are certain questions and matter of fact never presented to the public when the topic of so-called "passing for white" comes up? Consider the following:

- Hispanics and Arabs within the U.S. population show obvious signs of the supposedly dreaded "black blood." Puerto Rico, Cuba and the Dominican Republic are essentially mulatto nations. Nearly all Mexicans have some black ancestry from the African slaves who were brought to colonial Mexico and then assimilated into the Indian and mestizo populations. Why is there an "escape hatch" for Hispanics and Arabs when their Anglo and Creole counterparts are condemned as "light-skinned blacks"? Whites who are told by family members to consider themselves "black" are told that "society" or "whites" in general hate and despise the dreaded "black blood." But what racist worth his salt says that the "inferior" Negro blood is more than welcome into the white race as long as it comes speaking Spanish or Arabic?

- Since it is acknowledged that the "one drop rule" is racist, why are we told to preserve it instead of eliminating it? Why aren't the people accused of "passing for white" hailed as heroes who defied racism instead of being subjected to character assassination and the kind of condemnation usually reserved for child molesters and serial killers?

- Why are black American elites and black-identified mulattoes usually the most fanatical and enthusiastic supporters of the "one drop rule"? Indeed, could this racist myth even continue to exist in polite society if blacks turned against it?

- Why is evidence against the "one drop rule" ignored? Why is the public never told that the antebellum Southern states legally permitted persons with one-fourth to one-eighth "Negro blood" into the white race, and could be even more lenient when the person or family was accepted by the local white community? Why are we not told that the "one drop rule" is not related to slavery but accompanied the rise of Jim Crow segregation and the eugenics movement? Why is the audience not told that no American is legally obligated to call himself "black" and the "one drop rule" depends almost totally on self-policing? Why are they lying to us?

While the Jews of Europe were punished with physical genocide for supposedly "polluting the "pure blood" of the "Aryan race," Anglo and Creole Americans of partial black ancestry are subjected to documentary genocide and the lynching of reputations. People are declared "black" because some paper or ancestral document has the telltale words "black," "Negro," "Colored," or "mulatto." Or, like Anatole Broyard, their reputations are blackened after they are dead and can't defend themselves.

The web sites *Interracial Voice* and *The Multiracial Activist* have spent several years challenging the idea of hypodescent. This is the doctrine that the offspring of mixed race unions should always identify with the ancestral group with the lowest social status and never with the higher status ancestry. In those years we have learned many things about "race" in the United States.

American Indian Ancestry and White Racial Identity

All white supremacists hold that white racial purity is essential for the survival of the white race. The support of so-called anti-racists for the "one drop rule" complements this idea perfectly. If a drop of black blood can truly make a white person black, who can blame whites who are opposed to inter-racial marriage? Bigotry becomes self-defense. Yet, even here there are contradictions. American Indian blood is considered harmless and compatible with white ancestry in a way that black blood is not. We started to ask why an American can say, "My grandmother is an Indian but I am white," when he cannot say "My grandmother is black but I am white" without his right to a white identity being challenged.

All our lives we have seen people such as the late Johnny Cash, Burt Reynolds, Loretta Lynn, Cher, etc., proudly proclaim their American Indian ancestry without this acknowledgment being taken as a repudiation of their white ancestry or right to a white identity. One of Johnny Cash's records, called Bitter Tears, is devoted to denouncing the wrongs done to American Indians by that favorite villain of politically correct American history, "The White Man." But somehow Johnny's whiteness was not compromised by this. According to the letter of Virginia's Racial Integrity Act of 1924, most part-Indian whites would not be white, yet few Americans realize this. Why can't "black blood" be treated like American Indian blood? Why are *Interracial Voice* and *The Multiracial Activist* the only ones asking that question?

Have you noticed that, while Bell Curve-type studies purporting to show the genetic inferiority of blacks appear with some regularity, no one produces studies purporting to show that American Indians are racially inferior to whites? Could this be because the wide acknowledgment of American Indian ancestry in whites protects American Indians from this kind of racial attack? There is no political profit in it. In the two versions of the American movie, *The Squawman*, the American Indian wife of a British aristocrat is clearly presented as racially inferior, but their son is not. The son is even considered a worthy heir to his father's title and estates in

England. Change the wife's race to "black" and try to imagine that ending.

White Honor, Dishonor, and the Severing of Interracial Family Ties

Sociologist Orlando Patterson, in his cross-cultural study of slavery, *Slavery and Social Death*, describes a slave as a person with no ancestors. Biologically, of course, everyone has ancestors. But the slave has no official family and no family rights and obligations within society. He is socially dead. In American history, describing a physically white person as nonwhite, especially Negro or black, was a perfect way for white elites to send a message to the white masses: Don't get too close to or friendly with blacks or mulattoes. Otherwise, you will lose your race, your honor, your whiteness, your very ancestry. You will become socially dead to other whites.

The producers of the 1934 version of *Imitation of Life* worried about how they were going to present the "passing for white" girl without evoking the specter of miscegenation. Clearly, some "pure white" had to mate with a Negro for the girl to exist. How could they avoid reminding the audience of that? It is no accident that, in *Pinky*, *Imitation of Life*, *The Human Stain* and other anti-passing melodramas, you almost never see any parents or ancestors who look like the accused passer. We are told that the absent father of the "passing" girl of *Imitation of Life* fame was a "real light-skinned colored man" since her docile black mammy would never be so bold and uppity as to mate with a real white man. The point is that we are meant to see the girl as a genetic freak. Whites did not produce her, we are told, and therefore have no family responsibility to her. We are also told that her spiritual descendant, Anatole Broyard, had no white ancestors since there were no "pure" whites among his immediate ancestors. The same could be said for most Latinos, but somehow their lack of white racial purity doesn't count.

What is a family? What is an ethnic group? What are the obligations of a family? The "one drop rule" and the anti-passing drama tell us that the "passer" has sacred obligations to his socially inferior black-identified relatives which should prevent his upward mobility, but his "pure" white relatives have no obligation to him. Officially, he doesn't have any white relatives or ancestors. The very term "light-skinned," which has been used to describe anyone from brown-skinned people to Nordic blonds, is used as a euphemism to avoid saying "white." We are taught that the "passer" is "light-skinned" but not "white." Why? Because the word "white" implies a connection to and family relationships with white people - something anti-miscegenation laws and racial classification statutes were designed to destroy.

As previously mentioned, black elites and black-identified mulattoes have internalized many of these racist beliefs that "whites" and "blacks" can never be part of the same family. Yet, the Southern mulatto elite, which traditionally considered themselves the "superior" members of the "inferior" race, have families that are very racially mixed. The "one drop rule" or myth allows them the emotional luxury of hating whites in general while prizing the physical characteristics that white ancestry bestows. Most of the anti-passing hysteria in the post Civil Rights era seems to come from this group. Their fanatical devotion to the "one drop rule" is also used as a moral shield by others who want to promote the "one drop" or hypodescent ideology that proclaimed blacks and mulattoes inferior in the first place.

Hating Whites and Loving White Genes: Black Support of the "One Drop Myth" and White Racial Purity

In 1999 *The Washington Post* published an emotional article by one of its so-called "black" reporters, Lonnae O'Neal Parker, in which the author described her trauma when she discovered that her first cousin, Kim, was white-identified. This shouldn't have been too surprising since Kim was born to and reared by a "pure" white mother, looks totally white, and has a "light-skinned" mulatto father who was not keen to identify with blacks.

O'Neal Parker's article became a nationwide sensation. *The Seattle Times* and other papers reprinted it and ABC Television's *Nightline* devoted an entire episode to it. O'Neal parker's highly irrational thesis was that Cousin Kim and all others in a similar situation have an obligation to repudiate their white ancestry and identify with blacks in order to make up for any wrongs done to blacks and black-identified mulattoes by whites in both the present and the distant past. In other words, the "one drop rule" is presented to the public as a sign of black moral superiority instead of black biological inferiority. Cousin Kim supposedly chose the evil, racist whites over the innocent, pure-hearted blacks. This is also the way the "one drop" myth was justified in *The Human Stain* and the attacks on Anatole Broyard. O'Neal Parker, who is herself mulatto elite—not physically black but not as white as Kim—has no problem incorporating white genes into her family, but she does not want whites in it since whites are defined as the enemy. Only in *Interracial Voice* and *The Multiracial Activist* could one find some suggestion that O'Neal Parker's racial views were—shall we say—not a picture of good mental health.

We find it very interesting that O'Neal Parker insists that Cousin Kim must refuse to be white because "whites" are the enemies of blacks. It was the white-owned *Washington Post* and other white media that promoted O-Neal Parker's venom and let it go unchallenged. They were the ones who gave her a forum. In *The New York Times*, black columnist Brent Staples performs a similar task ; his columns are used mainly to promote the "one drop rule" and denounce "passing for white." The "one drop" myth is promoted either through blacks or justified as a glorification of blacks.

Racial Kidnapping and Ethnic Rape

What do we mean by a glorification of blacks? At *Interracial Voice* we started using the terms racial kidnapping and ethnic rape to refer to the practice of claiming as "black" people who were not physically black and did not identify with blacks. Kidnapping and rape are appropriate analogies here because the victims are taken by force—clearly against their will. Anatole Broyard was such a victim. Here are some other major examples:

Michael Morris Healy, an Irish immigrant, arrived in the U.S. around 1815 and established a plantation near Macon, Georgia. He took a mulatto slave, Eliza Clark, as his common-law wife and the two produced 10 children. All of the surviving children were sent North to be educated and protected from slavery since Georgia made legal manumission almost impossible. They were baptized as Catholics and lived the rest of their lives as proud Irish Americans. James Augustine Healy became Bishop of Portland, Maine. Patrick Francis Healy became President of Georgetown University from 1873 to 1881. Michael Morris Healy, Jr. joined the U.S. Revenue Cutter Service (the forerunner of the U.S. Coast Guard) and became a celebrated sea captain, the sole representative of the U.S. Government in Alaska. Now, many decades after their deaths, these proud (and "white") Irish Americans are being widely promoted as "blacks." First "blacks" this and first "blacks" that, even though no one identified with blacks could have accomplished what they did. The U.S. Government named an ice cutter after Captain Healy, but only to honor blacks, not him. Indeed, for Captain Healy it is an insult rather than an "honor."

What is the point of this racial or ethnic kidnapping? Does it prove what blacks could accomplish? No! The Healys were biologically more white than black and, socially, they were white. What can the public conclude except that something is strangely unique, mystical and inferior about black genes? (See http://www.interracialvoice.com/powell8.html)

On November 30, 1944 Calvin Clark Davis of Bear Lake, Michigan died a hero's death in World War II as part of the U.S. Army Air Force. He was posthumously honored with several medals. However, the "honor" was tainted by the fact that Davis was described as a "black man" who "pretended to be white." Indeed, Davis' racial identity has received far more publicity than his military heroics. I wrote an article about

Davis for *Interracial Voice* called "Pissing on the Grave of Heroes." Davis, we are told:

- passed for white
- lied about who he was
- concealed his race
- faked being white

Remember what I said about having no ancestors? Far from being honored for his military service, Davis is being publicly shamed and dishonored.

Another World War II hero "outed" for alleged "passing for white" was Pvt. Robert Brooks of Sadieville, Kentucky. He died heroically in the Philippines on December 8, 1941. His story appears in Studs Terkel's book on World War II, *The Good War*.

Here are other prominent examples of racial kidnapping or ethnic rape:

- Jean Toomer, whose name is taught to schoolchildren and college students as the "black" author of a book of poetry and short stories called *Cane*, was in fact a multiracial Caucasian who rejected a false "black" identity and wrote extensively on why the U.S. racial classification system should be eliminated in favor of a common "American" identity.

- Alexander Dumas, the French author of the famed novel *The Three Musketeers*, is presented to American schoolchildren as "black" when he was really three-quarters white and in no way socially "black."

- Alexander Pushkin, the greatest of Russian poets and father of Russian literature, is frequently presented to schoolchildren as another famous "black" because of one African great-grandfather.

Why are all of these people described as "black" in American schools even though there are no physical or cultural standards to justify that description? Are they claimed as "black" because of a tacit fear that "black" genes cannot stand on their own? Is this a "liberal" version of the old racist canard that miscegenation "improves" the "Negro" race while "degrading" the white race?

The Lies that Sustain the Myth of "Passing for White"

When the "one drop myth" is reported in the mainstream media, no mention whatsoever is made of the evidence against it. Such evidence, if presented, never sees the light of day and is limited to a few people who take pains to study the subject. The American people are not allowed to consider the following:

- If the "one drop rule" is real and enforced by whites, why is a glaring exception made for Hispanics and Arab-Americans? It does not take a genius to see both the physical and historical evidence that Hispanics and Arabs are nearly all "tainted" with the blood of what used to be America's official "inferior race."

- Why aren't Americans told that antebellum definitions of "white" tended to be more liberal than 20th century definitions; people with one-fourth to one-eighth Negro blood were legally allowed into the white race. For example, Eston Hemings Jefferson, the former slave son of Thomas Jefferson and Sally Hemings (and whose white descendants are the only Hemings descendants to pass a DNA test showing descent from the Jefferson line), was legally white once he was manumitted because he was at least seven-eights white. We should not be surprised that in both abolitionist and Republican Party literature, "white slaves" were frequently used to arouse the Northern white population against slavery. Why are these facts kept from the American people?

- What are the real world standards for saying that someone is "black" and not "white"? Eston Hemings Jefferson is always described in the media as "light-skinned black" who only "passed for white," but his

descendants are acknowledged as white without qualification. Where is the cutoff point? The only one I can
see is that dead whites with a touch of the dreaded
"tarbush" are "black" and those still living are
'white."

In the magazine *American Heritage*, a white woman
named Jillian Sim announced that she had discovered that her
great-grandmother was Anita Hemmings, a white mulatto or
mixed white who graduated from Vassar College in the late
19th century was almost expelled for being "colored" when a
wealthy and envious classmate decided to have her background investigated. Now Vassar proudly claims that Anita,
who lived as white for the rest of her life, was their first
"black" graduate. Jillian Sim accepts the myth that Anita was
a "black" who "passed for white" and she condemns both her
paternal grandmother and great-grandparents as "blacks" who
"passed for white." Sim, her father, and her son, however, are
still white. The dead are "black" and the living are "white."

After Broadway star Carol Channing's recent disclo-
sure that her father was partially black but lived all his life as
a white man, you'll notice that Channing is not described as
"black" in the media but her father is described that way without qualification. Moreover, if you look at the Amazon.com
comments on Channing's autobiography, *Just Lucky, I Guess*,
you'll note that commentators who are black-identified insist
on calling her "black" as well.

People as diverse as the actress Mae West, former
U.S. President Dwight David Eisenhower and former Georgia
Congressman Bob Barr, etc. have been labeled "black" (usually by blacks and black-identified mulattoes) on the basis of
the one-drop myth. There appear to be no standards except
opportunism—the ethnic rape charge again.

It is common, we at *Interracial Voice* have discovered, for black-identified supporters of the "one drop" myth to
announce that people don't "look white" when they've been
white all or nearly all of their lives. They will shamelessly insist that Carol Channing doesn't look white and Mae West
didn't look white. They could see the dreaded colored blood

all along! Mixed whites who used to travel all over the Jim Crow South as white, are told by fanatical black-identified folks that they are obviously black. These rants are so similar, we swear there must be a school somewhere that teaches black-identified folks nothing but defense of the "one drop" myth.

"Passing for White" is an Honored American Tradition—for Nearly Everyone Else.

"Passing" is an honored American custom for nearly everyone except tarbrushed whites—non-Hispanic, non-Arab whites and mulattoes who have the misfortune to be too American or Louisiana Creole. It is not so much your touch of the dreaded black blood that matters, but whether or not your ancestral documents (census records, birth, marriage and death certificates, etc.) bear the telltale words "mulatto" or "free person of color" or "Negro" on them.

The Latino escape hatch. Throughout most of the 20th century, Latino elites in the United States (and the government of Mexico itself) argued that all Hispanics should be classified as "white" on all official records—regardless of appearance or ancestry. So a blond person with the "tarbrush" could be labeled "Negro" in Texas while a dark-skinned Mexican with no white blood or European ancestry would be officially labeled "white"—even if he was treated more like a Negro than a white person. Now that is big time passing!

South Asians. Before the Civil Rights era and the rise of affirmative action, South Asians from India, Pakistan, etc. insisted that they were "white." They were first labeled "non-white" and then received the ultimate honor of being called "white." According to this myth, dark-skinned people from India were dark-skinned "Caucasians" while "tarbrushed" Americans of totally European phenotype were unworthy to call themselves "Caucasian." Now South Asians are called "Asians" and are eligible for "minority" benefits and the numerous advantages "white guilt" can bestow. Big time passing!

Mississippi Chinese. The Chinese of Mississippi started out as "colored" and many of the men married "Negro" women. The leaders of the Chinese community begged the local white elites for the right to be classified as "white" instead of "colored." The price the white elites imposed was rejection of all Chinese kin who were part-Negro or intermarried with Negroes. Big time passing and a rejection of family that you will never see condemned on television a la *Imitation of Life*.

Jew and "Passing for White." The Jewish immigrant moguls who founded Hollywood prided themselves on rejecting their Jewish heritage and forced Jewish actors and actresses to change their names. That is why Jews named Issur Danielovich, Bernie Schwartz and Betty Persky became Kirk Douglas, Tony Curtis and Lauren Bacall, respectively. You can buy books telling you about hundreds of famous Americans who are secretly Jewish. By "secretly" I don't mean that they would deny it if you asked them. I mean that they don't announce it and carefully present a non-Jewish image to the public. This is called passing when the tarbrushed whites do it. It is big time passing!

Working Class "Passing." Hiding a working class background when one rises in class is considered morally acceptable. In an anthology of autobiographical essays from academics from the working class, *This Fine Place So Far From Home: Voices of Academics from the Working Class* (Temple University Press, 1995), editors C.L. Barney Dews and Carolyn Leste Law present a stream of stories in which academics from poor and working class backgrounds quickly learn to "pass" as upper middle class in origin and hide their less desirable relatives and backgrounds. In the 1930's movie, *Stella Dallas*, the working class mother drives her daughter away so the girl can be reared by her upper class father and have a better life. The film ends with the mother secretly looking at her daughter's high society wedding while standing outside in the rain. Imagine *Imitation of Life* ending like that! Big time passing!

Southern Whites in the North and "Passing for Yankee." One can also say that Southern whites who move North quickly learn to drop the accent and "pass" for Yankee. I once asked Rick Bragg, the former *New York Times* reporter and author, who is from Alabama, how he managed at *The Times* when he is so obviously Southern. He admitted that he is an exception. Many others will not deny that they were born south of the Mason-Dixon line, but hope to God that no one brings it up. Think of it! How many white Southerners do you know who are not poor and living in a community with other Southerners who retain their accents or advertise their Southern origins? Big time passing!

Finally, how can there be true equality in this country while the "one drop" myth is presented to the American people as a perverted ideal we must honor—for no reason that makes any sense? I began this presentation with a reference to racial definition laws of Nazi Germany. There is no sense in pointing out the illogic and racism of the Nuremberg Laws while simultaneously upholding the "one drop" myth and its assumptions of white racial purity.

We at *Interracial Voice* and *The Multiracial Activist* have spent years arguing with people (the vast majority of them black-identified) who claim to be devoted opponents of racism but fight like hell to retain the myth that all true whites are "pure" and "one drop" of "black blood" makes you "black." But what we call "race" is a spectrum of human colors and phenotypes that blend into each other. There are no hard and fast boundaries that divide one so-called "race" from another. Whenever we fail to challenge the "one drop" myth and argue in favor of human freedom to choose one's one own identity, we effectively deny that sacred reality.

II. "White," "Mixed" or "Other"?
Some Books and Articles
Your Librarian Didn't Tell you About!
Originally published in *Interracial Voice* at
<http://www.interracialvoice.com/powell.html>

White by Definition: Social Classification in Creole Louisiana **by Virginia R. Dominguez, Rutgers University Press, 1986.** Dominguez is one of the few serious researchers in the area of racial mixture and white racial identity. She shows the importance of individual choice in overcoming the legal manipulations and bogus statutes of the power elite. She is also one of the few scholars honest enough to see the connection between the Hispanics and non-Hispanics of interracial ancestry. Indeed, she notes that the use of the term "Hispanic" as a racial category is designed to help government avoid dealing with the reality of racial intermixture.

The Forgotten People: Cane River's Creoles of Color **by Gary B. Mills, Louisiana State University Press, 1977.** Mills shows the higher than expected status that mixed-blood Creoles had in antebellum Louisiana (as does Dominguez in *White by Definition*). Remember that whenever you hear references to "black" plantation owners in the antebellum South, someone is trying to steal history from racially mixed people (mulattoes, quadroons, etc.) and give it to blacks.

"Miscegenation and the Free Negro [sic] in Antebellum 'Anglo' Alabama: A Reexamination of Southern Race Relations" by Gary B. Mills in *The Journal of American History*, Vol. 6, No. 1, June 1981. Pp. 16-34. Check pages 27 through 31 of this long article and you will see where Mills shows that families of known racially mixed ancestry moved from "colored" to "white" status within a generation or two with the knowledge and consent of the white community. This information totally contradicts the myth of "passing."

Race and Kinship in a Midwestern Town: The Black [sic] Experience in Monroe, Michigan, 1900-1915 by James E. DeVries, University of Illinois Press, 1984. DeVries plainly states that the white community of Monroe, Michigan accepted the mobility of part-black whites into the white community. This again contradicts the "passing" myth. DeVries, however, is too much of a "liberal" racist to admit that and offend black elites. He even goes so far as to suggest that the white community of Monroe was "racist" for accepting part- black whites into the white community. Damned if you do and damned if you don't! A quote from the book:

> Crossing over was not the silent mechanism that some historians have indicated. It involved not only racial heritage but, ironically, family and personal identity. Could an individual known to have an African ancestry be regarded and defined as white? Yes, the interracial backgrounds and unions of the Fosters and Duncansons were matters of public knowledge. Each of the families had a long, continuous heritage in Monroe, and descendants residing in the community today bear no stigma of race and are generally viewed as Caucasian. (P. 150)

Black [sic] Masters: A Free Family of Color in the Old South by Michael P. Johnson and James L. Roark, W.W. Norton and Company, 1984. Johnson and Roark found that a "white mulatto" member of a "free colored" plantation-owning family served in the Confederate Army with the full knowledge and acceptance of the white community. "White" status seemed to be more closely related to loyalty issues rather the strict "purity." (p. 307).

Racial/Ethnic Groups Who Also Faced the "Are They White, Colored, or Whatever?" Question. In Other Words, the People Mixed-Race Anglos are Always Accused of "Passing For," are Mixed Too.

Anglos and Mexicans in the Making of Texas, 1836-1986 **by David Montejano, University of Texas Press, 1987.** Montejano describes the great inconsistencies in defining Mexicans as either "white" or a separate "race." Mexican-Americans faced segregation similar to a Jim Crow system. The recent PBS series *Chicano!* also illustrates this fact. The existence of a racially mixed ethnic group with numerous racial phenotypes and class distinctions confounds the efforts of white elites to establish clear racial boundaries. Mexicans are a mixture of Indian (predominately), Spanish and black (from the slaves brought to colonial Mexico by the Spanish). Though they usually fail to mention the third element in their ancestry, many Mexicans have clearly Negroid facial feature and hair texture.

"Colored and Catholic: The Lebanese in Birmingham, Alabama" by Nancy Faires Conklin and Nora Faires in *Crossing the Waters: Arabic-Speaking Immigrants to the United States Before 1940*, edited by Eric J. Hooglund, Smithsonian Institution Press, 1987. This article relates the efforts of Lebanese immigrants in Alabama to establish "white" status and make themselves an exception to the Jim Crow laws. The Lebanese were too dark for their claim to "white" status to go unquestioned. You might say they were unknowing victims of the degradation of "Anglo" mulattoes.

Strangers from a Different Shore: A History of Asian Americans **by Ronald Takaki, Little, Brown and Company, 1989.** Takaki states that "In 1909 federal authorities classified Armenians as "Asiatic" and denied naturalized citizenship to Armenian immigrants." Armenians had to go to court to have themselves declared "white." South Asians also were denied "white" status due to their dark skin colors (despite the efforts of Anthropologists who claimed that skin color in "Caucasians" range from very pale to very dark brown or almost black).

Pocahontas: The Evolution of An American Narrative by Robert S. Tilton, Cambridge University Press, 1994. Tilton explores the role of Pocahontas and the "Indian Princess" legend in creating white elite identity and legitimizing the stealing of Indian lands. The claim of descent from an Indian Princess is very popular among many whites. Tilton argues that is a way of saying that we didn't steal the land but inherited it. Here is an interesting quote from Tilton:

> ...for many base wretches amongst us take up with negro women, by which means the country swarms with mulatto bastards, and these mulattoes, if but three generations removed from the black father or mother, may, by the indulgence of the laws of the country, intermarry with the white people, and actually do every day so marry. Now, if instead of this abominable practice which hath polluted the blood of many amongst us, we had taken Indian wives in the first place, it would have made them some compensation for their lands. ...We should become rightful heirs to their lands and should not have smutted our blood.... – The Rev. Peter Fontaine of Virginia, 1757.

Mixed-Bloods and Tribal Dissolution: Charles Curtis and the Quest for Indian Identity by William E. Unrau, University Press of Kansas, 1989. Unrau relates how mixed blood or "white Indians" were promoted by government as a "civilizing" influence on real or full-blood Indians. Charles Curtis is often listed as an "Indian" (1/8) Vice President of the U.S., but he was fully "white" in every caste or social sense. We should ask what is the difference, if any, between a "mixed blood Indian" and a part-Indian "white?" What is the role of a "mixed" elite (for either Indians or blacks) in reinforcing ideas of white superiority and institutions of white supremacy? Indeed, whenever blacks insist on claiming people who aren't of Negroid phenotype for their "race" aren't they really expressing an inferiority complex and a tacit belief that their genetic stock needs to be improved with the blood of their hated but adored white "enemy?"

When Jesus Came, the Corn Mothers Went Away: Marriage, Sexuality and Power in New Mexico, 1500-1846

by Ramon A. Gutierrez, Stanford University Press, 1991.
This is an excellent study of racial intermixture in New Mexico under colonial Spanish rule and the early days of the Mexican republic. Check out this passage regarding the origin of the word "mulatto":

> Professor John Nitti of the University of Wisconsin's Medieval Spanish Dictionary Project informs me that the word *mulato* initially meant a racial mixture of any sort. Offspring of Spaniards and Moors were known as *mulatos* in medieval Iberia, as were later mixtures between blacks and Indians, and between Frenchmen and Indians. Eventually *mulato* came to mean specifically a mixture between a black and a white. *Mulato* appears in New Mexican church records, though there is no evidence that the individuals classed as such had any black African ancestry.

Here's a passage that reminds us of many of today's Latino leaders:

> Don Pedro Pino, New Mexico's representative to the 1812 Cortes at Cadiz, reported to that assembly that "In New Mexico there has never been any caste of people of African origin. My province is probably the only one in Spanish America to enjoy such distinction." Don Pedro was patently wrong, but advanced the claim to validate a myth he wished to perpetuate, namely that New Mexico's nobility had preserved their honor and racial purity over the centuries.

***Slaves Without Masters: The Free Negro in the Antebellum South* by Ira Berlin, Vintage Books, 1974.** This book **should** be called "The Free Mulatto or Multiracial...". However, Berlin would never have won the National Historical Society Book Award if he had been that honest. Most of the "free colored" caste could be called multiracial as opposed to "black." The best thing about Berlin's book is how he details the antebellum laws that acknowledged varying admixtures of black ancestry in the white population (as opposed to the "one drop" rule that really had its origins in the 20th century). Here's an interesting passage:

> Fearful of pushing too many persons of both colors to the wrong sides of the color line, the South Carolina legislature never legally defined the Negro and left the problem of distinguishing between mixed-bloods and whites up to the courts. South Carolina

jurists generally drew the line between white and black at somewhere between a quarter and an eighth Negro ancestry, but they
also made legal passing contingent on social acceptability as
well. ... Allowing the question of whiteness to turn on public acceptance as well as genealogy enabled many well-placed whites
to free their mulatto children from their proscribed status.

***Mexican Americans: Leadership, Ideology, & Iden-
tity, 1930-1960* by Mario T. Garcia, Yale University Press,
1989.** This is a really interesting history of Mexican American
political leadership and its quest to fight racial discrimination
against Mexican-Americans while pretending to be a pure
"white" ethnic group. The League of United Latin American
Citizens (LULAC) constantly went to court arguing that position. However, you'll never see them denounced for "passing"
by black or liberal elites.

***Slaves of the White God: Blacks in Mexico, 1570-
1650* by Colin A. Palmer, Harvard University Press, 1976.**
The author details the black slavery in Mexico and the ancestry that Mexicans and Mexican-Americans pretend doesn't exist.

***Between Race and Ethnicity: Cape Verdean Ameri-
can Immigrants, 1860-1965* by Marilyn Halter, University
of Illinois Press, 1993.** Struggle of Cape Verdean (Portu-
guese/African) Americans to establish their identity in the
United States and their relationship with "white" (still pretty
dark) Portuguese.

***The Melungeons, The Resurrection of a Proud Peo-
ple: An Untold Story of Ethnic Cleansing in America* by N.
Brent Kennedy with Robyn Vaughan Kennedy, Mercer
University Press, 1997.** The origins, persecution and re-
emergence of a Southern multiracial ethnic group. Kennedy
provides fascinating accounts of the politics of racial classification.

***Creoles of Color of the Gulf South* edited by James
H. Dormon, University of Tennessee Press, 1996.** How multiracial Creoles have maintained their ethnic identity despite
oppression.

***The Shadow of Blooming Grove: Warren G. Harding
in His Times* by Francis Russell, McGraw-Hill, 1968.** This

book is interesting to students of racial classification because of the racist smear campaign conducted during Harding's presidential campaign in 1920—that he was part Negro. Russell provides fascinating detail on this campaign, an issue that the Harding family is still sensitive about. Harding won anyway.

The Sweeter the Juice: A Family Memoir in Black and White by Shirley Taylor Haizlip. Simon and Schuster, 1994. Haizlip starts out as a devoted believer in the "one drop" myth who wonders why she and her mother are the only "white" members of her "black" family. She decides to trace her mother's missing relatives, imaging them to be "blacks" who are "passing" as white. She's forced to change her mind as she encounters white relatives who remain "white" despite the revelation of their partial black ancestry. Haizlip herself moves more toward a multiracial as opposed to a purely "black" identity.

The Lives of Jean Toomer: A Hunger for Wholeness by Cynthia Earl Kerman and Richard Eldridge, Louisiana State University Press, 1987. Falsely labeled as a "black" author because of his book of poetry and short stories, CANE (which deals almost exclusively with multiracial people), Toomer fought a life-long battle to be recognized for what he truly was. His theories of a "universal man" beyond racial demarcation makes him an important dissenting voice against the hypodescent status quo. Also see The Jean Toomer Pages at <http://www.math.buffalo.edu/~sww/ toomer/jean-toomer.html>.

Desegregating the Altar: The Josephites and the Struggle for Black Priests, 1871-1960 by Stephen J. Ochs, Louisiana State University Pres, 1990. Readers should know that there is a movement among black and liberal American Catholics to create a "black Catholic" history that rightfully belongs to multiracial Americans. Louisiana Creoles are the victims of this attempt to create "black" Catholics, but the most prominent victims are three brothers born to an Irish-American father and a mulatto mother in antebellum Georgia. James Augustine Healy was bishop of the diocese of Portland,

Maine from 1875 until his death in 1900. Patrick Francis
Healy served successively as professor, prefect of studies,
vice-rector, and, from 1874 to 1882, as rector of Georgetown
University. Alexander Sherwood Healy served as rector of
Holy Cross Cathedral and, for a few months before his death
in 1875, as pastor of St. James Parish in Boston. Ochs admits
that the Healys did not identify with blacks but with their Irish
heritage and were not considered "black" by others. Indeed,
not only were the Healy brothers only one-quarter "black" and
of caucasian phenotype, but it was their Irish father who
reared them as Catholics and paid for the educations that allowed them to rise to such high positions in their Church.
Nevertheless, hypodecent fanatics like Ochs claim that
"blacks" deserve all the credit.

    The Mississippi Chinese: Between White and Black
by James W. Loewen, Harvard University, 1971. Loewen
describes how the Chinese moved from "colored" to "white"
in Mississippi by agreeing to the demands of the white elite
that they cut all ties with part-black Chinese and those married
to "colored" wives. You'll never see the Chinese denounced
for "passing" in black or liberal publications.

    Chinese in the Post-Civil War South: A People With-
out a History **by Lucy M. Cohen, Louisiana State University Press, 1984.** How the Chinese used their in-between
status to intermarry with both whites and "colored" in the
South.

    White by Law: The Legal Construction of Race **by
Ian F. Haney-Lopez, New York University Press, 1996.**
How is "white" defined in the U.S.? The definition varies tre-
mendously. Lopez concerns himself mainly with immigration
issues and how East Asians, South Asians, Latinos, Armenians, Arabs and others made legal efforts to prove themselves
"white" in order to gain U.S. citizenship.

    Making Ethnic Choices: California's Punjabi Mexi-
can Americans **by Karen Isaksen Leonard, Temple University Press, 1992.** When men from India's Punjab province
were not allowed to bring women with them from India due to
racist immigration laws, they intermarried with Mexican

women. A multiracial Punjabi-Mexican American ethnic group was the result.

On Gold Mountain: The One Hundred-Year Odyssey of My Chinese American Family **by Lisa See, Vintage Books, 1996.** The author describes how her multiracial Chinese and European American family thrived in Los Angeles, California despite anti-miscegenation laws. Marriages between family members of Chinese ancestry and "whites" were conducted in nearby Mexico and then the couples moved back to California. California obviously did not prosecute couples who evaded its anti-miscegenation laws the way Southern states did.

The Temple Bombing **by Melissa Fay Greene, Addison-Wesley, 1996.** The title refers to the infamous bombing of Atlanta's oldest and most prominent synagogue on October 12, 1958 by white supremacists. However, the book is also a social history of Southern Jews, their marginal position in Southern race relations, and their constant fear that their "whiteness" (the "passing" theme) could be challenged.

Scenes in Red, White, and Black: The Eugenic Assault on America **by J. David Smith, George Mason University Press, 1993.** Smith shows the 20th century link between anti-miscegenation laws and the eugenics movement. Forced sterilization of the institutionalized, racial registration and restricting miscegenation were all linked to the idea of "improving" the [white] gene pool. The best part of the book is the hidden history of the minority of fanatical racial purists who wanted to ban all non-Caucasian ancestry (with the exception of small amounts of American Indian ancestry possessed by white elites such as the descendants of Pocahontas) from the white "race." Special emphasis is placed on Virginia and the men whose names are unknown but should go down in infamy: Walter Plecker (who headed Virginia's bureau of vital statistics and delighted in hunting down "impure" whites and Indians) and Virginia aristocrat John Powell of the Anglo-Saxon Clubs. Showing the link between black nationalism and white racism, Smith details the friendship between John Powell and Marcus Garvey (both believed in promoting racial purity).

The Ramapo Mountain People **by David Stephen Cohen, Rutgers University Press, 1974.** Also called "Jackson Whites," this is the story of a multiracial community of Dutch, Indian and black ancestry that has existed since colonial times.

Ambiguous Lives: Free Women of Color in Rural Georgia, 1789-1879 **by Adele Logan Alexander, University of Arkansas Press, 1991.** While the author slavishly subscribes to hypodescent, she provides good historical detail on how the privileged social and educational opportunities of Southern multiracials were due to their often close ties with whites fathers and other relatives (as opposed to the myth of the callous white rapist slavemaster "breeding" more slaves). These privileges created the myth that mulattoes and mixed-whites were the "flower of the colored race." These "mulatto elites" filled the "Negro" colleges and universities and reinforced the idea that intelligence comes from "white blood." When you recognize this history, you can see why the NAACP makes the ridiculous claim that losing non-blacks to a "multiracial" category will somehow destroy all the progress that "blacks" have made. Many of them probably still have the tacit belief that intelligence comes from "white blood."

Woman of Color, Daughter of Privilege: Amanda America Dickson, 1849-1893 **by Kent Anderson Leslie, University of Georgia Press, 1995.** This book should be read with *Ambiguous Lives*. The biography of an "elite mulatto lady" who inherited her white father's plantation and became the richest "colored" woman in the U.S.

Indian Slavery in Colonial Times Within the Present Limits of the United States **by Almon Wheeler Lauber, reprinted by Corner House Publishers, 1970.** This work, originally published in 1913, proves that extensive Indian slavery existed side-by-side with Negro slavery in colonial America in virtually all the colonies.

Lumbee Indian Histories: Race, Ethnicity and Indian Identity in the Southern United States **by Gerald M.**

Sider, Cambridge University Press, 1993. The history of the Lumbee Indian tribe of North Carolina (now officially the largest Indian tribe east of the Mississippi) should be required reading for the study of racial intermixture in the United States. Listed as "free colored" (a generic term for "nonwhite") during the antebellum period, they fought a long and constant battle against the state of North Carolina for the right to call themselves "Indians" instead of "Negroes."

Powhatan's Mantle: Indians in the Colonial Southeast, **edited by Peter H. Wood, et. al., University of Nebraska Press, 1989.** This book also deals with Indian slavery. Important mention is made of uneven sex ratios among Indian and early black slaves, with women predominating among the former and men among the latter. Black and Indian intermixture probably far outnumbers black-white intermixture. Colonial merchants waged slave-raids against Indian tribes and "An inestimable number of Indians from many tribes found themselves either being shipped away as slaves from colonial ports or working as slaves in and around them."

The Only Land They Knew: The Tragic Story of the American Indians in the Old South **by J. Leitch Wright, Jr., The Free Press, 1991.** Emphasis on Indian slavery and intermixture with whites and blacks.

Southeastern Indians Since the Removal Era, **edited by Walter L. Williams, University of Georgia Press, 1979**. Good essays on the history of the Lumbees of North Carolina, the Houma of Louisiana, the Catawba of South Carolina and the Indians of Virginia in their struggle for ethnic survival and dignity within a white/black Jim Crow dichotomy.

Slavery and the Evolution of Cherokee Society, 1540-1866 **by Theda Perdue, University of Tennessee Press, 1979.** *The Cherokees: A Population History* **by Russell Thornton, University of Nebraska Press, 1990.** *Creeks and Seminoles* **by J. Leitch Wright, Jr., University of Nebraska Press, 1986.** The three books listed above contain important information on the social and legal implications of Cherokee intermixture with whites and blacks.

The Deaths of Sybil Bolton: An American History **by Dennis McAuliffe, Jr., Times Books, 1994.** This book provides valuable information regarding the legal status and psychology of mixed-blood "white" members of Indian tribes. The author, a journalist, started out by investigating the death of his maternal grandmother, who was part-Osage Indian and an enrolled member of the tribe. Concentrate on the history and ignore the author's attempt to impose a "one drop of Indian blood" rule on himself and his family—using the "one drop of black blood" myth to justify it. I note that in the many book reviews that appeared when the book was first published, McAuliffe's historical research was praised but no one took his claim of being a white "Indian" seriously—quite the opposite of what happens when whites claim to be "black" (e.g., Gregory Howard Williams).

The Life and Death of Okah Tubee **edited by Daniel F. Littlefield, Jr., University of Nebraska Press, 1988.** This book is an introduction to the autobiography of a Choctaw Indian who was enslaved as a child. The book is marred by Littlefield's racist introduction, in which he insists on referring to Tubbee as a "black" passing for "Indian." Littlefield claims that Tubbee was born to a black slave mother and a white father who emancipated the mother and two older children, who later became prosperous members of the "free colored" community, but kept Okah Tubee (then called Warner McCary) as the slave of his own mother and siblings. Littlefield, in his devotion to hypodescent, does not want to consider that Tubbee was most likely a Choctaw slave trying to claim his lost heritage.

Long Lance: The True Story of an Imposter **by Donald B. Smith, University of Nebraska Press, 1982.** This story is fascinating history as long as you ignore the racist ("black" passing for Indian) remarks of the author. Long Lance (born Sylvester Long) was born in North Carolina of Indian, white and black ancestry. If his ancestry had been Indian and white only, Smith would praise him to the skies for seeking out his Indian heritage. Smith, however, insists throughout the book that Long was only good enough for his small amount of black ancestry. Long Lance launched a career as a journalist and gained fame as a provocative writer and eloquent speaker for the cause of the North American Indian.

The Lumbee Problem: The Making of an American Indian People **by Karen I. Blu, Cambridge University Press, 1980.** How the multiracial people now called the Lumbee Indians of Robeson County, North Carolina fought the state's attempts to classify them as "Negroes" and finally achieved recognition as Indians. Fascinating details on how Robeson County depends upon associations and social ties to "define" people since phenotype and "black blood" cannot be depended upon to determine racial classification in the county.

Africans and Native Americans: The Language of Race and the Evolution of Red-Black Peoples **by Jack D. Forbes, University of Illinois Press, 1993.** Forbes, a prominent scholar of Native American studies, explores the evolution of racial terminology and the changing meanings of racial terms such as "black," "mulatto," and "mestizo." Forbes emphasizes the constant racial mixing that has occurred throughout the centuries between Native Americans, Africans and Europeans.

Pocahontas's People: The Powhatan Indians of Virginia Through Four Centuries **by Helen C. Roundtree, University of Oklahoma Press, 1990.** What is especially interesting to students of racial classification is how Virginia's Racial Integrity Act of 1924 (its infamous "one drop" law) was used to persecute Native Americans.

Many Tender Ties: Women in Fur-Trade Society, 1670-1870 **by Sylvia van Kirk, University of Oklahoma Press, 1980.** *The New Peoples: Being and Becoming Metis in North America* **edited by Jacqueline Peterson and Jennifer S.H. Brown, University of Nebraska Press, 1985.** The two books listed above are excellent histories of the origins, flowering, persecution and resilience of Metis (European and Native American) society in both Canada and the northwestern U.S.

Robert Stafford of Cumberland Island: Growth of a Planter **by Mary R. Bullard University of Georgia Press,**

1995. Robert Stafford was a wealthy Georgia planter who had several children by mulatto women and provided handsomely for them. The book provides fascinating information on how wealth could socially "whiten" people of known multiracial ancestry.

Poor Relations: The Making of a Eurasian Community in British India, 1773-1833 **by Christopher Hawes, Curzon Press, 1996; may be purchased from University of Hawaii Press.** The Anglo-Indians were created by intermarriage and mating between British soldiers and Indian women. As early as the 1830s, Eurasians (later called Anglo-Indians) already exceeded the number of British civilians in colonial India. At the time of India's independence, they outnumbered **all** British residents. Yet, there has been little historical attention given to the development of this mixed-race community, to the problems that it faced (social, economic and attitudinal), nor to the questions that its rise posed to British authority.

Hawes describes how the mixed-race experience in India is typical of the "European colonial adventure" worldwide. The social and legal experiences of mixed-race people is influenced by class status (especially the father's status), birth within marriage versus the stigma of bastardy (British discrimination against people born outside of wedlock was especially harsh), and the conflict between the law and family ties. Hawes' research shows that the British as individuals had no real qualms about interracial marriage and, contrary to the hypodescent rule, wanted their biracial offspring to be British. The problem lay with British elites whose devotion to the new "scientific" racist doctrines resulted in oppression typical of the mixed-race experience:

- The mixed-race communities are utilized to maintain colonial authority but denied the highest offices reserved for "pure" whites (with a few exceptions for multiracial persons of great wealth).

- The colonial power fears that the mixed-race community will present a challenge to "white" authority and blur the lines between the "superior" European and the "inferior" non-European.

- The mixed-race community (especially its educated elites) maintains its ambition to be treated as part of the European caste, but is subject to laws that prevent a full identification with the ruling nation to which it is bound by blood and culture.

Eurasian populations...undermined, in the most public manner possible, concepts of colonial rule which depended ultimately on maintaining the illusion of the racial superiority of white European males. The consequent dilemma for Eurasian populations was how they might identify fully with their parent colonial societies, on which they were economically dependent and to which they were culturally bound. They shared in what has been termed the `imagined community' of nationalism as fully as their European fathers and forefathers, but were denied participation on equal terms. In turn the predicament of colonial authority was how far should it go in acknowledging its children of mixed race. In practice it seems that there was an uneasy compromise in colonial societies between disavowal and acceptance. Parental responsibility and considerations of Eurasian utility to the regime were in tension with concepts of Eurasian political unreliability and the damage which full acceptance might do to perceptions of white prestige.

***Degas in New Orleans: Encounters in the Creole World of Kate Chopin and George Washington Cable* by Christopher Benfey, Alfred A. Knopf, 1997.** Benfey spends less time on the famous French painter Edgar Degas and the alleged influence that New Orleans and his Creole relatives had on his work than he does in relating the story of one of Degas' relatives: a brilliant "quadroon" engineer named Norbert Rillieux who invented an efficient steam-driven apparatus for refining sugar.

When you ignore Benfey's racist use of the term "black" to describe people who are far from it, you find important information about the privileges and oppressions experienced by mixed-race Creoles in 19th century New Orleans. Rillieux (who is often falsely listed as a "black" inventor) was a highly respected professional whose predominate white ancestry allowed him to utilize his talents in a way that would not have been possible if he had been black.

One of Rillieux's close friends and major supporter in Louisiana sugar circles was Judah P. Benjamin, the Jewish Confederate luminary who later served as Jefferson Davis's Secretary of State. In a nice touch of irony, Benfey compares the image of the "mulatto" in American literature with that of the "Jew" in European literature:

> Almost white, almost free, "oriental," and effeminate, at once wealthy and a social pariah, the free man of color in his literary depictions occupies much the same place as the Jew in literary Europe. (The first article of the eighteenth-century "Code Noir," or Black Code demanded the expulsion of the Jews from New Orleans.) Jews and free men of color were difficult to detect; they often LOOKED like white citizens, and passed for such. It was against the radical "otherness" of Jews and free people of color that the proper Englishmen and proper Louisiana Creoles respectively sought to define their own uneasy identity.

III. A Political Alliance Among ALL Multiracial/Multiethnic Individuals!?

Originally published in *Interracial Voice* at
<http://www.interracialvoice.com/powell2.html>

[A.D. Powell's assessments should be required reading for "blacks," academicians, "white" "liberals" and especially Latinos. Eloquently stated and entirely necessary. – William Javier Nelson, author of *The Racial Definition Handbook*]

An alliance between all groups and individuals who have suffered because of the refusal of government elites to recognize the legitimacy and normalcy of interracial ancestry is certainly desirable. The obstacles to such an alliance, however, are cultural and political and these differences must be aired.

The main victims of "one drop" mythology have been the mixed-blood descendants of "whites" (however that is defined) and those blacks from the American ethnic group that was formerly enslaved in the United States (predominately in the South). While Southern elites took pains to stigmatize intermixture in order to confirm their doctrine of black racial inferiority, most of the propaganda promoting the "one drop" mythology has come from black and mulatto elites and their "white liberal" allies. Unlike avowed racists, they stressed their supposed belief in racial equality while expressing absolute panic at the thought of "white blood" escaping from the Negro "race." The tacit assumption was that "white blood" was the source of intelligence and beauty (especially beautiful women) and that mulattoes and Creole whites would perform great deeds in the name of the Negro, thereby "proving" that race's equality with whites. The latter statement is a contradiction, but human beings are nothing if not contradictory.

Enforcing the "one drop" mythology has, ironically, depended almost totally on self-policing. Not even the dreaded South had a system designed to "hunt" impure whites as the Nazis hunted Jews. Racial classification trials tended to focus more on "reputation" rather than proof of "impurity." Southerners may have been racists, but they were not total fools. They knew well that "the tarbrush" could happen to any white person, and it was best to not look too far into another white's background. The task of truly policing "white purity" fell to the black and mulatto elites. It was their job (which they performed with great enthusiasm) to scare mulatto and Creole whites within their families into thinking that the entire white race had met and blackballed them from the fraternity. Novels and films that condemn "passing" (a racist term implying that the offender is destroying white "purity") are inevitably produced by blacks and mulatto elites (mulattoes who consider themselves the elite of a "race" that includes blacks).

In contrast to the above, the government has gone to great pains to hide the tri-racial ancestry (Indian, black and white) of Latinos. The Census Bureau was ordered to classify them as white (regardless of looks or genetic background), and they were not segregated in the armed forces (despite skin colors as dark as that of any black). Despite these privileges obtained from the federal government (which didn't want to admit that Latin America is racially mixed), Mexicans and Puerto Ricans were discriminated against by ordinary people and local governments (which refused to ignore their dark skin). Latino elites have often looked the other way when the "one drop" myth is being discussed, pretending that they aren't involved (Ray Suarez of National Public Radio's "Talk of the Nation" is a Puerto Rican (i.e., mulatto) and a prime offender). Also, most Anglos of mixed ancestry don't get to meet Latinos and see the "one drop" myth being openly violated.

Indian/white intermixture has an inherent contradiction. We have all seen Westerns in which the "half-breed" is denigrated and the Indians alone are described as his/her "people." However, we also know that many "whites" openly proclaim Indian ancestry (Johnny Cash, Loretta Lynn, Will Rogers, Burt Reynolds, Cher and many, many others) while claiming total membership in the white "race." Such people have often discriminated against Indian/black or Indian/black/white people by banning the latter from tribal memberships. The "white Cherokees," for example, brought slavery to the Cherokee nation in order to have workers for their plantations and banned Cherokees mixed with black from the nation. They also were enthusiastic supporters of the Confederacy whose states had kicked their tribes out of the Southeastern U.S. Whenever you hear Cherokees whining about the "Trail of Tears," remind them of this!

The truth is that most Americans are not concerned with "racial purity" but government elites are concerned with promoting the myth that they are. Latinos and Arab-Americans often clearly show black ancestry but are not forced to call themselves "black." I have seen many Italians, Jews, Greeks, etc. who are supposedly of "pure" European descent but look like mulattoes. Europe itself is not "pure," especially Southern Europe. If you remind academic and political elites of this, they will quickly change the subject because they know they are lying when they claim a "white" consensus for the "one drop" mythology. Indeed, if black elites stopped advocating "one drop" mythology, I give it a year to disappear altogether!

In summary, an alliance between all "mixed" groups is necessary and can come about if some individuals take the lead. However, they must all denounce "one drop" mythology, white racial "purity," and show solidarity with each other.

IV. A.D. Powell vs. Marc Eisen
Originally published in *Interracial Voice* at
<http://www.interracialvoice.com/powell3.html>

The more I live on this earth the more convinced I am
that "one drop" propaganda is almost SOLELY attributable to
black elites and so-called "white" liberals. Black elites give
"permission" to social-climbing so-called "whites" to attack
Creole whites and light mulattoes as "black" and not good
enough for their white ancestry. The liberals get the chance to
indulge in ego-boosting racism against an unprotected group
while pleading "not guilty" to any charges of racism because
they are only quoting from black elites and "blacks," they
claim, are always right on "race." At the same time that liberal
elites join black elites in demanding that Creole whites like
the late New York Times book critic Anatole Broyard (attacked in The New Yorker magazine as "black" and only
"passing for white") confess to every passerby every drop of
magical (i.e., "inferior") "black blood," these same liberals
take great pains to hide THEIR "inferior" Jewish, Slavic, Hispanic (a group whose racial mixture is not acknowledged),
Mediterranean, etc. ancestry. Consider the following excerpts
from a racist article against Anatole Broyard by a racist "liberal" editor who wants his own ancestry to remain unknown:

Excerpt of "Life in Black and White" by Marc Eisen,
"Liberal" and self-described "white" editor of the "liberal"
Madison, WI news weekly, *Isthmus*, July 12, 1996. After a
long piece of ego-boosting whining because a clerk was nice
to him and he's certain she would have been nasty to him if he
had been black, Eisen says:

Black remains the all-powerful, indelible adjective.

Of late, no better illustration of this reality can be found than
Henry Louis Gates' New Yorker profile of Anatole Broyard, the
late New York Times literary essayist. I had always imagined
Broyard as a quintessential Gotham intellectual, no doubt Jewish,
a product of City College, and so on. Wrong. Broyard was a
light-skinned black (sic) man from New Orleans whose family
had migrated to New York in the 1940s.

Gates investigates the essential riddle of Broyard: Why did he
deny his blackness [sic]? Why didn't he tell his own children?
How did his secret inform his writing? The answer, Gates suggests, is that Broyard understood, in the context of America's hy-
persensitivity to race, that the label "black" would forever stereotype his writing.

So Broyard chose to shroud his racial heritage and construct a
new identity (how typically American). He even ended contact
with his darker-skinned sister, As a Village intellectual on the
make, he owned a bookstore, wrote for Commentary and Partisan
Review, hung out with Alfred Kazin and all the lit-politick lions
(Eventually, though, he traded the Boho life for a series of upper-
class Connecticut homes and even a day job at an ad agency before joining The Times.).

But never, never, did Broyard willingly 'fess up to his blackness,
not even to his grown children as he lay dying, painfully, of pros-
trate cancer. For Broyard, life was a matter of self-invention—not
"authenticity" as the promoters of identity politics believe.
Broyard wanted to be known as a writer, not a Negro writer. "His
perception was perfectly correct," Gates writes sympathetically.
"In a system where whiteness is the default, racelessness is never
a possibility."

This is an essential truth of America in the 1990s. We kid ourselves to believe that America has arrived as a color-blind society. Yet, astonishingly and to our peril, we seldom talk about it."

My letter to *Isthmus* http://www.interracial-
voice.com/edit@isthmus.com printed in the August 23 issue:

Editor:

Is Marc Eisen running for Fuhrer?

I'm not kidding. If the late New York Times book critic Anatole
Broyard had been guilty of child molesting instead of "rasen-

schade," Eisen would have treated him with far more respect ["Life in Black and White," July 12].

The "crime" that Broyard committed, in the eyes of Marc Eisen, is the same "crime" that Jews were alleged to have committed during the reign of the Third Reich. Even though German Jews looked and acted like other Germans, the Nazis alleged that they were really a separate "race" of "impure blood" who were really only inferior imitations of "Aryans" and not entitled to call themselves German at all. Eisen's attack on Broyard says the same thing, except that he uses "black" for "Jew" and "white" for "Aryan."

What is Eisen trying to prove? He knows that millions of people in this country de-emphasize or fail to mention Jewish, Slavic or other ethnic ancestries, poor or working-class backgrounds, etc. in order to either rise in the world or exercise the individualism and self-determination which are supposedly at the core of the American character. The federal government's traditional way of dealing with the racial mixture (Indian, black and white) that characterizes the Hispanic population was to "pass off" or declare all of them "white" regardless of racial phenotype. Now what was Broyard's "crime" again? Being a white guy who called himself white? By the way, does Marc Eisen recite his genealogy to everyone?

Marc Eisen used to spend his time attacking powerful elites who were guilty of abuses that harmed real people and the public interest (the privatization of HEAB, for example). Now he's reduced to attacking a dead man for "rasenschade." Broyard's honor is untarnished but the same can't be said for Marc Eisen's.

A.D. Powell

Reply from Marc Eisen:

Dear Mr. Powell,

How could you misread my column as badly as you have? Are you dense or just tendentious?

The point of it, which should have been abundantly clear to you, is this: America is horribly hung up on race. Despite the successes of the civil rights laws, blacks are often treated differently than whites in both large and small ways.

To cast me as a Nazi for pointing this out is beyond belief.

You castigate me for "attacking" Anatole Broyard yet make no mention of the fact that I was citing Henry Louis Gates' profile of Broyard in the New Yorker. I can only conclude that you are a willfully dishonest person for (a) trying to besmirch me for something that Gates wrote and (b) for horribly misrepresenting Gates' point—that black people haven't been assimilated into the American mainstream, unlike Jews, Italians, and other ethnics. The Gates profile, if anything, is sympathetic to Broyard for having to go to extremes (i.e., denying his blackness) in order to be judged by his writing alone rather than his skin color.

I don't know what planet you're operating from.

With great disdain,
Marc Eisen

P.S. Yes, we will run your letter.

My reply to Eisen's letter:

Actually, my last letter was very friendly, giving Eisen the benefit of the doubt. Perhaps he is merely ignorant instead of an evil social-climber trying to make himself whiter by destroying the reputation of a dead man. Obviously that is not the case. Eisen tries to assign to Broyard a false "black" racial identity that is meant to be the ultimate insult. How would Eisen react if his right to call himself "white" were questioned? Indeed, doesn't Eisen take great care not to "insult" the Hispanic or Arab with Negroid features by calling them "black." I have met Jews and Italians who claimed "pure" European ancestry and had the suspiciously Negroid looks that Broyard didn't have. Wasn't Broyard whiter than they are?

Both Eisen and Henry Louis Gates are jealous of Anatole Broyard. Gates is jealous because he wishes he had Broyard's whiteness and ability to assimilate. Eisen is jealous because he wishes he had Broyard's literary fame. He cannot stand the thought of a man from an ethnic group he despises (the multiracial Louisiana Creoles) achieving the fame and respect that has alluded him.

Both Gates and Eisen hate the fact that Broyard was accepted as white by friends who knew of his "impure" ancestry and those who "suspected" didn't care. This certainly makes them the moral superiors of Eisen and Gates.

Eisen claims that Jews, Italians, etc. are assimilated. The Far Right would dispute him on that. The German Jews were deemed to be perfectly assimilated until the Nazis placed upon them the same charge that Eisen and Gates use to condemn Broyard: The charge that they were an inferior, separate race that looked like Germans, spoke like Germans but were not good enough to be German. The Nazi analogy holds and anyone who cannot see it is either ignorant of history or deliberately blind. Eisen is too great a fool to realize that, in utilizing the myth of white racial "purity" to attack Broyard, he is giving strength to an ideology that can be used to destroy innocent people from any ethnic group—not just the ones despised by Marc Eisen.

Instead of uniting with Gates, Tina Brown of The New Yorker and other social-climbing hyenas attacking Broyard's corpse, Eisen should humbly sit at the feet of others and learn wisdom.

Another reply from Eisen, just as stupid as the last one:

Dear Mr. Powell:

What is your problem?

You've apparently fallen down the rabbit hole, eaten a strange substance and created a magical world in which up is down, black is white, and fantasy is reality. I'm at a loss to connect your ravings to what I said in my column.

One more time: The column discusses how extraordinarily racially sensitive America is and how black people in large and small groups are treated unfairly by the majority culture. Despite the extraordinary accomplishments of the Civil Rights laws, we continue to be, fundamentally, a racially divided society.

I conclude: "This is an essential truth of America in the 1990s. We kid ourselves to believe that America has arrived as a color-blind society. Yet, astonishingly and to our own peril, we seldom talk about it.

Having bizarrely ignored the main points of my article, you've fixated on the idea that Anatole Broyard wanted to be identified as a Creole. THERE IS NOTHING IN HENRY LOUIS GATES' PROFILE THAT SUGGESTS BROYARD HAD ANY SUCH DESIRE. You've concocted this out of thin air!

You have, in your fevered imagination come to believe I said Broyard committed a "crime" by denying his black heritage. You bizarrely continue to assert that I want a race-based society. You somehow assert I feel that Broyard isn't good enough to be white. I think you're hallucinating.

For reasons I don't understand, you've inverted the meaning of my column and accused me of the very thing that I've tried to spotlight—America's tragic hang up with race.

You're a crank lost in your fantasies.

With disdain,
Marc Eisen

Eisen carefully ignores these facts:

1) He followed a traditional, racist attack line used against mixed whites in which the racist states that the "inferior Negro blood" makes them too leprous to be "whites" but the "white blood" would make them a "superior" variety of "black." If Eisen is totally ignorant of the tradition he is following, then he has no business lecturing people on "race."

2) Eisen studiously ignores the evidence explaining why the "one drop" myth if not truly enforced (Hispanics and other groups) and the example from Holocaust history of what happens if you endorse the concept of "invisible" race and the "racial purity" of the dominant "race."

3) Eisen (like other "America is so racist" liberals I've known) insists that putting down "uppity" mulattoes and Creole whites is merely a statement of his love for blacks and that anyone who supports the right of mulattoes and Creole whites to be "white" or otherwise non-black is denying the existence of racism in the United States—both past and present. This neat trick is designed to silence debate on an issue they personally fear—the white race's lack of "purity."

4) Eisen (like other "blacks-can-do-no-wrong" liberals) denounces Broyard for enjoying white-skin privilege, but Eisen wants to keep the same privilege for himself. Eisen's column goes so far as to deny Broyard's physical whiteness altogether, implying that he shared the same "color" as Gates. Eisen denounces Broyard for not announcing his "inferior" drop of blood to every passerby (like the Biblical leper shouting "Unclean! Unclean" so others would not be contaminated by his touch), but Eisen has never, in all the years he's been

editor of Isthmus, informed his readers of HIS ancestry. Passing is fine for Eisen but not for Broyard.

5) Your enemy is always the person who wants to deny and denounce you for the very things he himself practices. Eisen is a racist enemy of the multiracial community and probably the social climber he accuses Broyard of being. If he were 1/10 as antiracist as he claims to be, he would denounce "white purity" and note the shared ancestry, social situations and other commonalties between many ethnicities that are recognized and those that are yet to be recognized. Eisen is 100 times more dangerous than any avowed racist because he (along with Gates) misleads people of good will and tells them that you must go against your conscience and embrace white "purity" and the "one drop" mythology in order to be antiracist.

V. The Problem With Gregory Howard Williams: Poster Child For The "One-Drop" Myth Of White Racial Purity

Originally published in *Interracial Voice* at
<http://www.interracialvoice.com/powell4.html>

It is no accident that Gregory Howard Williams, a very white man who proclaims himself to be "black," has received far more television and newspaper publicity that all the people in the multiracial identity movement put together. Williams, Dean and Professor of Law at the Ohio State University College of Law, is being lionized by black and liberal elites who are presenting his autobiography, *Life on the Color Line: The True Story of a White Boy Who Discovered He Was Black*, as the ultimate statement on "race" and racial intermixture in the United States.

Williams has appeared on national television programs such as "Larry King Live," "The Oprah Winfrey Show," "Dateline NBC" and ABC's "Nightline." His book has even been made into a motion picture for Fox-TV and will soon enter the homes of millions of Americans to preach the gospel of hypodescent and the "one drop of black blood" myth of white racial "purity." No one who challenges the hypodescent mythology comes close to gaining this kind of extensive publicity. No books that seriously explore the variety of the multiracial experience, such as the anthologies of Maria Root and Naomi Zack, have been promoted by national bookstore chains and reviewed in almost every newspaper in the country.

Williams is a polished orator with an emotional, dramatic delivery. Every guilt-ridden liberal in the audience is moved to tears as he vividly describes:

- His idyllic "white" childhood in Virginia and the day his "light mulatto" father took Williams and his brother on a bus to Muncie, Indiana and told them that they were really "colored."

- How his "white" grandmother called him "nigger."

- How Williams and his brother were beaten and rejected because they were too "white" for the blacks and too "black" for the "whites" after they dutifully followed their father's instructions to identify themselves as "Negroes."

- How his father never made more than a thousand dollars a year after returning to Muncie because he was "black."

- How Williams swore he would become an attorney and "make something of himself" to prove that "blacks" are not "inferior."

- How "society" forced him to be "black" and he "had no choice" once his dreaded black blood was revealed.

But . . . here's what Williams and his supporters won't mention:

Latinos and other partially African-descended minorities and how they openly "get away" with refusing a "black" identity in a nation where most "whites" are supposedly obsessed with white racial "purity." Does the presence of Latinos prove that most "white" Americans are NOT obsessed with white racial "purity" and Gregory Howard Williams and his supporters are lying? Williams also describes his "white mulatto" father, Tony Williams, as "passing for" Italian or Greek because of the darkness of these "white" ethnicities. But why are these "white" ethnic groups so dark? Could it be

because of their geographical closeness to Africa and their ancestors' intermixture with Africans? These are questions that
Williams and his supporters don't want anyone to bring before
the public.

His father's self-destruction. Why did Tony Williams
choose to return to Muncie (the only city where he had left a
"colored" reputation) when he had the entire United States to
choose from? Wasn't Williams' father typical of "black-
identified" non-blacks in that he policed himself and his family to enforce the "one drop" myth when no outside force or
person could have done it? Williams takes great pains to tell
every audience about the time his "white" grandmother called
him "nigger" but usually fails to mention that Tony Williams
was the first to describe his son in such a disgusting way. Williams loves to tell his audiences that his father was wealthy in
Virginia because he was "white" there but never made more
than a thousand dollars a year in Muncie because he was
"black." Bull! Tony Williams was a drunk, a wife beater
(which is why Williams' "white" mother took the two younger
children and left), a poor businessman (who didn't know what
to do when a nearby military base closed and his tavern began
to lose money), a child abuser who took his sons from their
home and deposited them in a ghetto slum with his alcoholic
mother, and a lazy bum who just decided to stop working and
wallow in self-pity. The senior Williams was a "white" man in
the 50s when there were plenty of jobs. Hell, coal-black men
were making good money in the auto factories and other un-
ionized industries. Tony Williams was not "black"—he was a
sick SOB.

Williams ignores the role of social identification as
opposed to genetics. He called his mother a racist for aban-
doning him and his elder brother, but doesn't explain why this
"racist" married Tony Williams with full awareness of his
mixed ancestry and produced four children with him. Williams doesn't explain why his mother raised his two younger
siblings as "white" even though they had the same paternity
and dreaded "black blood." Williams delights in telling of the
privileged summers he spent with his maternal grandparents

in Muncie, describing to a tearful audience how his grandparents later rejected him when he became "colored." Why doesn't Williams expect us to ask the obvious questions? Since his mixed ancestry (apparently known to all the adults in his family) was acceptable with a "white" identity, it is apparent that the "black" identity came from accepting that designation and acting as an "inferior." Tony Williams allowed his inferiority complex to "choose" a "black" identity for himself and his minor sons. It is apparent that the cowardice of the mother and grandparents in not rescuing "Greg" and his brother from their abusive father originated in their fear that the boys had accepted the "nigger" identity Tony Williams had chosen for them. If the problem had been Greg's "black blood," he wouldn't have been acceptable before.

By promoting the "one drop" myth of "no choice," Williams has done far more than any self-described racist to oppress people of mixed racial ancestry who have the "misfortune" to have some traceable black ancestry but do not have the great privilege of being Latinos (an ethnic description which supposedly cleanses the "taint" of "Negro blood"). It is extremely hard to point out the racist nature of the hypo-descent myth when people who paint themselves as opponents of racism are the biggest supporters of the myth.

If, for example, anyone uses the word "Aryan" in a racial sense, it's not only Jews and other groups that were victims of the Third Reich's genocidal policies that will take pains to set him straight. By contrast, black elites and some of their "white" allies take great delight is assassinating the character of multiracial Caucasians such as the late New York Times book critic Anatole Broyard, describing him as a mere (by implication) "black" who presumed to call himself "white" despite his Caucasian phenotype and predominate European ancestry. Very few people who claim to be anti racist will defend Broyard (and, by implications, all other part-black non-Hispanics who reject a "black" identity) because they dare not contest with blacks regarding what is and is not racist. No self-styled "progressive" or conservative defends "Aryan" racial terminology but many of them defend the "passing for white" myth because they have been exposed to blacks (and those who claim to be "black") who are its enthusiastic supporters.

Williams is now on the defensive. He claims he is being persecuted by a "multiracial police" out to destroy his "right" to be "black." Really? When he appeared with Ted Koppel on "Nightline," Williams claimed he had no choice in being "black." The "multiracial police" are not supposed to point out this contradiction.

Williams has a right to tell his story or call himself what he pleases, but he has a moral obligation to cease using his story to terrify others into the black fold when they don't want to be there and don't HAVE to be there. Williams has a moral obligation to make the following points in all his interviews and personal appearances:

No one is legally or socially required to call themselves "black." The presence of Latinos in this nation is proof that "black blood" does not preclude identification with other racial labels including multiracial, Indian, Asian, mestizo or even that "godlike" appellation "white" (which the blasphemous Anatole Broyards of this country have dared to claim).

Williams should cease referring to himself as someone who found out he was truly "black," or describing his "true legacy" as "poor and black." He should cease referring to his mulatto or multiracial father as a "light-skinned black" (that is an oxymoron).

Williams is not simply selling his autobiography. He is promoting the "one drop" myth and that is why he has received so much publicity. If Williams had lived the same tragic childhood but ended up calling himself "white," "multiracial," or any label other than "black," do you believe for a moment that he would have received even a tiny fraction of the publicity with which he has been showered? Black and liberal elites know what they're doing. Williams is a club they use to frighten and beat "white blood" into the "black" fold.

Gregory Howard Williams—a simple black and white mind advocating a simple black and white world. It would be ludicrous if it the stakes were not so high and the suffering so great.

VI. White Folks: A True Story
Originally published in *Interracial Voice* at
<http://www.interracialvoice.com/powell6.html>

"Is the stupid woman crazy or what? How could she
do such a thing to an innocent—and perfectly white—baby?"
The nurses at a hospital in a large, Northern city were
shocked. "The woman's white as anyone else—whiter than
many, to tell the truth, and she's insisting that the baby's parents be listed as 'colored' on the birth certificate! Insane!"

The woman herself, like most of her ilk, enjoyed the
look of shock on the faces of others when she voluntarily
dived from the most "superior" race in the world to the most
"inferior" one. True to her type, she had developed a maso-
chistic devotion to her stigma, her inferiority, her taint of "inferior blood." Just as she hated herself, she had to hate every-
thing that came from her. Later, the child she hated had that
birth certificate corrected to "white." It was easy. Like most of
her ilk, the woman and her husband constantly contradicted
themselves and married as "white" in a deep South state. But
that's another story.

It's said that the cross-cultural definition of a slave is
"one who has no ancestors." That was certainly true of this
woman. The pictures of her and her brother show blond, blue-
eyed "Aryan" children—the kind the German S.S. used to
steal in order to breed the "master race." Instead, they were
adopted by a stupid Caucasian woman who believed she
wasn't good enough for her own European ancestry (even as
she secretly took pride in it) and her dark mulatto, professional husband. Instead of breeding the "master race," their
destiny would be to "improve" the world's most "inferior"
race with the "superior" blood of that race's hated but adored

enemy. Like other white captives, their "superior" European
blood would, they were told, be used to "prove" the "inferior"
race was not truly inferior. Of course that's a contradiction,
but no one is supposed to notice that.

Who were her parents? Legend has it that her mother
was a Hungarian immigrant. Who was her father? God alone
knows, but he MUST have been tainted with the most inferior
of all bloods. Otherwise, the adoption agency would NEVER
have allowed the adoptive parents to submit white children to
the ultimate social injustice. Decades later, contrary to the social workers' gospel, "white" families delighted in adopting
such fair and "tainted" children. They didn't see anything
wrong with them. Social workers from a certain "race" pan-
icked. "Racist" whites who didn't have sense enough to know
how "inferior" certain blood was supposed to be, were taking
the "superior" blood an "inferior" race needed to "improve"
its stock. Such "racists" had to be stopped and the social
workers did. But, back to our story.

"Why did my mother give me up?" She echoed the
words of every adopted child from time immemorial.

"Well, I suppose she didn't want you. You're tainted
with inferior blood, you know. She was too good for you,
that's why you ended up with us." The childless Old Lady and
her husband had achieved the dream of their mulatto elite
caste. As self-styled "superior" members of the "inferior" race
and "beautiful" members of the "ugly" race, they could claim
as their own the beauty of the "superior" race and plead not
guilty (on a technicality) to the dreaded miscegenation. Like
other members of their caste, they delighted in introducing the
children as their own. "Whites? What whites? Don't you think
WE can produce pretty blond babies too? What do whites
have to do with it?"

Puzzled "whites" in a large Midwestern city and later
in Southern California scratched their heads in amazement.
What's going on here? Non-white minorities who prided
themselves on not identifying with a certain race were even
more puzzled. "I'd give my right arm to be that white, to trade
this dark skin for the whiteness they needlessly repudiate,"

said the Mexican, the Filipino, the Asian Indian, the Chinese, etc. "Those people are really stupid!" Wherever the mulatto elite caste and their black masters go, they take pains to teach the doctrine of inferior blood to those who don't know it. "Excuse me, but I'm not as good as you think I am. I may look white and superior, you see, but I'm unworthy of the honor of my own ancestry because I'm tainted with the blood of an inferior race. You didn't know that? Happy to keep you informed." That could be the mulatto elite motto. It's their religion.

The children began to have real problems, the daughter especially. She often ran away from home. These children were not going to bring glory to the "inferior" race, despite their abundance of "superior" blood. Throughout her life, she was to have temper tantrums and was once institutionalized for mental problems. Who are you? What's YOUR ethnicity? She had no answer to those questions? The psychiatric report described her as an "inferior" female with "very light skin" as if she were an albino or a genetic freak. Obviously THEY couldn't cure what ailed her. There were other curious bits of her history. The principal of her Chicago high school has once called her adoptive parents to complain that she was "trying to steal the boyfriends of the Jewish girls." Historically, Jewish girls aren't all that "white" and the Third Reich had murdered the relatives of these girls for the crime of polluting a "superior" race with their "inferior" blood. However, the daughter didn't know that. Without ancestors, without knowledge of herself and others, she was totally disarmed.

For a brief time, the daughter joined the army. There she met a handsome young Caucasian man who was also without ancestors. He was a lieutenant and she was a private. Now, officers aren't supposed to fool around with enlisted personnel. However, the powers that be on this deep South army base decided to look the other way. It solved an embarrassing problem. Nevertheless, a certain deep South state recorded the marriage of two white people, nationality "Americans."

The marriage didn't last long. The wife was mentally unstable and the husband was ambitious. He would use the military socialism of Uncle Sam (the only "socialism" or handouts considered respectable in the U.S.) to rise in the ranks, get an education, acquire the class status that would supposedly make up for the fact that he had no ethnicity. He had no word that would explain what he looked like and why he was the way he was. The only word that he felt he had permission to use didn't describe him.

Understand now that the young man could easily have joined the army without this stigma, as could his bride. However, like so many white captives, they could not see the forest for the trees. If no one has ever shown you how to do a simple thing, if you have no role models who can teach you to survive in the world with your dignity intact, chances are you will constantly overlook opportunities and snatch defeats from the jaws of potential victories. So it was with our young couple.

The divorce was bitter—even as divorces go.

"The bitch lied to me! She told me she was pregnant, then we married and she really got pregnant. I never wanted to get married!"

The wife screamed, screamed and screamed again.

The husband was still in love with his German girlfriend. They had even had a baby girl who didn't survive infancy. The wife could never compete with the sweet-tempered "pure" Aryan overseas—even if she had NOT been mentally unstable. Why didn't he marry the German? Perhaps he was afraid he would be getting above himself.

Our less than perfect couple had their own baby girl. The wife tried to commit suicide several times. She even turned the gas on and tried to kill both herself and the baby. The husband was stationed in the Orient. Neighbors smelled the gas in time and called the cops.

The husband was now stuck with a helpless infant. Men aren't supposed to take care of infants by themselves. Everyone knows that. What should a man do with a baby? Dump it on his mother! He headed South on a Delta airplane (what else?). The stewardesses and all the other women he encountered were charmed by the handsome young lieutenant with the cute little baby and no woman to help him.

After a year or so, a nasty custody battle followed. It took a lot for a mother to lose a custody battle in those days. You had to be mentally unstable AND whore around. Actually, it was not the wife who really wanted the toddler. It was her adoptive mother who wanted another cute, blond kid to show her relationship to the "superior" race without being brave enough to proclaim it.

Now the young ex-husband might have been forgiven for leaving his child with his mother for a short time. But he was busy with his army career, his travels and his girlfriends. He left the child in hell. No one except a white man with no ancestors would have been so senseless and ignorant.

To fully tell this story, we should probably go back into the 19th century. The young father never knew his grandparents. Indeed, there was a tacit but firm communication that he was not to ask about his father's background, nor about the many relatives who seemed to have "disappeared" without a trace. Intellectually, he knew that he was a descendant of the European race, but that race and those ancestors were too good for him. It's a common idea, and many who claim to be crusading against "racism" are still fanatical proponents of it because it caters to the inferiority complex of a certain politically powerful but socially insecure group of people.

By the time the child reached school age, purgatory had turned into hell. The young father forgot the torments he himself had suffered and did not realize how much worse it would be for his child, being both female and with almost no children like herself left in the town. What makes it even worse is the fact that it was all so unnecessary. The child could have lived with him on military bases with other dependents in a somewhat civilized environment, instead of enduring years of the following:

"What that white gurl doin here?"

"Let's beat up the white girl!"

"White people ain't no good! Dey crackers, y'all."

It would have been better if the child had at least been acknowledged as part of the race for whose sins she was being tormented. Is it surprising that later in life she developed a special contempt for those who try to deny that such hatred is INTERracial. Inwardly, she knew she did not belong to this race or this people. She always knew that one day she would leave it and go where she belonged. It is common to hear both liberals and conservatives worrying about white children losing their racial identity in predominately black schools. Curse them! Did they ever worry about the white captives and the deliberate attempts to destroy THEIR white racial identity? Let the "pure" kids suffer!

The teachers, like most adults, tried to ignore reality. When the children asked why a child of the hated enemy was amongst them, the teachers gave vague replies such as "Well, not everyone's exactly the same color." The teachers, being educated, knew what the children did not. "White" people may be their enemy, but it was an "honor" for their "inferior" race to assimilate as much of the enemy's blood as possible. It was a source of beauty and intelligence.

Black hatred for whites is strongly coupled with black lust. The child experienced both. She was very lucky she wasn't sexually raped, though she and all white captives are ethnically raped and racially raped. This kind of rape involves having an identity that is not truly yours forced upon you against your will. It involves the assumption that you have a moral obligation to be used as a source of European breeding stock in order to "improve" an "inferior" race. Indeed, that is the source of the Negro and mulatto elite outrage against so-called "passing." The rape victims are escaping from their tormentors; the white slaves are escaping from their black masters; "superior" white blood is like genetic gold and they are being "robbed" of it.

It's common for liberals to say that only dumb crackers think that black males lust after white women. Yes, they often do. The worse ones, however, are those who plead "not guilty" to the dreaded miscegenation by the technicality of the "one drop" myth. Show us a Southern town where people haven't heard versions of the following:

"Yeah, I wants to marry me a Creole. They got that long pretty hair. I don't want no nappy-headed nigger woman."

"I wants me a high yella. It just like f___king a white woman."

If the cracker boys come around and demand, "Nigger, what you doin with that white woman?" the nigger can just say:

"Lordy, boss, dis gal ain't white; she inferior like I is."

"Oh, sorry, nigger."

"Damn, fellas, that sure is a pretty white girl. It don't seem right." You see, even the people who supposedly created the "one drop" myth (actually, elites did) are puzzled and disturbed by its contradictions.

There is, of course, a more refined version of the above that may be called the racial trophy wife syndrome. In those cases, more refined, intelligent black males seek out mulatto and Creole white females as "beautiful" appendages to professional success. It is understood that "white" is beautiful and "black" is the opposite. They also get to deny that they are committing "miscegenation." This may be the real reason that their intelligentsia, who claim the moral right to tutor America on what is and is not "racism," fight like hell to maintain and perpetuate a "one drop" myth that condemns their genes as the most inferior, damning and undesirable on God's earth. What is even more hypocritical is the fact that these same people often condemn those who make "official" interracial marriages as lacking in "racial pride." They are really projecting their own racial inferiority complex onto others. The Indian and the Asian have more sense and more self-esteem. They do not attempt to claim people who are obviously not theirs, nor do they write and speak in favor of doctrines based on the assumption of their inferiority. This is why you will never see a "Bell Curve" revelation of the "inferiority" of American Indians despite their pitiful performance in schools and universi-

ties. The open acknowledgment of Native American ancestry
in "whites" makes that option politically unfeasible. One
would think the Negro and mulatto elites would learn, but
they are wedded to the fear that they might really be biologically inferior and "white blood" will somehow protect them
against the day. Why do you think the NAACP really pan-
icked when the multiracial category was proposed? Voting
rights? Bull! They feared losing "superior" white breeding
stock and the intelligence and (female) beauty that supposedly
comes with "superior" white blood.

The black and mulatto elite intelligentsia get the
Northern liberals to cry and feel guilty over the alleged rapes
they suffered during slavery. For those of you who claim that
personal experience is always superior to historical research,
let us say that personal experience would dictate that the Negro was "honored" not "raped." Outraged? Many peoples
have been raped throughout history. That is nothing new.
What is special about the Negro is the way he came to prize
the blood of the people he hated. No one fights to preserve a
shame; they do fight to preserve an honor. That is why the
Negro and his mulatto and white slaves foam at the mouth like
rabid dogs at the thought of captives escaping (i.e., "passing").
They fear the loss of "superior" blood. If the black and mulatto elite intelligentsia were honest in their inferiority complex, they might propose the following monument, to be
placed next to those omnipresent Confederate memorials in
every Southern town:

> To the Unknown Rapist
> Whose Superior Blood Gave
> Intelligence and Beauty to
> A Grateful and Inferior Race
> Sure, it's sick but it's honest.

Meanwhile, the child retreated into an inner world of
books, music and solitude. Her culture was not theirs, even as
her race was not theirs. One day she would escape.

VII. Harold McDougall at "Multiracial Identities & The 2000 Census" Panel
Originally published in *Interracial Voice* at
<http://www.interracialvoice.com/powell7.html>

I encourage *Interracial Voice* readers to view Harold McDougall's performance at the "Multiracial Identities & The 2000 Census" panel on C-Span (5/30/98, ID# 106489, 1-800-277-2698, $29.95 plus $7 shipping).

It is my strong OPINION that Harold McDougall is a sneaking, lying s.o.b. He is obviously a "hired gun" retained by the NAACP to assassinate the Multiracial Identity movement.

Harold states that a "multiracial identity" will not end "racism," therefore there should be no recognition of multiracial identity. Apply that to other identities. Latino rights, gay rights, women's rights, etc. will not end "racism" (which is being continually redefined so that things we used to consider flaming liberal are now being denounced as "racist" and "right-wing"), but would Harold and his NAACP confederates dare to say that those other movements should disband or put their needs aside until "blacks" have achieved "paradise" (by the NAACP's definition of the term)?

Harold says that interracial marriages will do nothing to "end racism" because married people still argue and therefore social problems will remain. This is similar to argument #1, in that the movement must achieve some vaguely defined version of paradise or be labeled a failure or irrelevant (a condition the NAACP would not dare to impose on any other movement). This is also similar to the frequent argument that racial intermixture has been "tried" and "failed" because ante-

bellum concubinage, Latin American intermixture, the South
African "colored" caste, etc. failed to achieve racial "paradise." The dishonesty here falls into two parts:

First, a society in which racism has been officially repudiated and (most) racial discrimination outlawed (the current U.S.) will supposedly become like societies in which racism was never repudiated and racial discrimination was legal
and mandatory simply because multiracial ancestry is officially recognized. This is impossible. The NAACP and its allies are implying that racial mixture was the cause of racial
discrimination—a ridiculous contention that cannot be supported.

Second, McDougall and his ilk deliberately fail to dis-
tinguish between interracial marriages in a society of legal
equality with concubinage and casual encounters in societies
where racial hierarchies were legally mandated. Interracial
marriage does not "end" but does DECREASE racism because family relationships are openly acknowledged and legally recognized. Interracial mixture in societies where interracial marriages were outlawed were burdened with legal re-
strictions that encouraged the denial of family relationships
precisely because elites feared that marriages would break
down the racial hierarchy.

Harold and his allies constantly emphasized the importance of "looks" and the opinions of people with whom
one has casual encounters (such as cab drivers). Of course, if
Tiger Woods is "black," because he "looks black," then
Mariah Carey is definitely "white" because she "looks white."
Of course, the NAACP doesn't want to say the latter. The
truth is that Latinos, Indians (both American and from India),
darker Europeans, etc. are constantly mistaken for the people
the NAACP wants to claim as "black" (just as Anglo multiracials are constantly relating how they are "mistaken" for Hispanic). Most "racial" identifications of people who are not
very "white" or very "black" depend upon a variety of social
clues. If a guy who looks like Tiger Woods is seen hanging
around the Chicano Studies office, most people will assume
he is Chicano. If he is hanging around the South Asian Studies

office, then he must be of Indian or Pakistani origin. If the Pakistani kid is seen at the mall, most people will assume he is Hispanic. When the Indian customer hands his credit card or check to the clerk and she sees an Indian name, she knows that she was mistaken and Mr. Singh is not Mexican or whatever identity she had casually assigned to him. The NAACP would never have the nerve to say that Latinos or South Asians should change their identities because some clerks or cab drivers think they are "black" because of their dark skin.

If the multiracial identity applied only to multiracials who are NOT partially "black," you can bet the rent that the NAACP would have no objection to it.

If no one had expressed concern about the biracial baby of that Danish actress being left in a stroller outside the restaurant in New York City, and something had happened to the child because no one called the authorities, you can be sure that Harold McDougall would be denouncing the "racism" of people who did not intervene to protect a helpless biracial infant. Damned if you do, and damned if you don't. McDougall and his ilk are afraid that there isn't enough racism to put "uppity" multiracials in the place the NAACP has assigned to them. That's why he's grabbing at straws and repeating this Danish woman's story over and over.

VIII. When Are Irish-Americans Not Good Enough to be Irish-American? "Racial Kidnapping" and the Case of the Healy Family

Originally published in *Interracial Voice* at
<http://www.interracialvoice.com/powell8.html>

Consider the following family history:

Michael Morris Healy, an Irish immigrant, arrives in the United States around 1815 and establishes a plantation near Macon, Georgia. Healy and his mulatto common-law wife, Eliza Clark Healy, have 10 children. All of the children are sent North to be educated, baptized as Catholics, and leave any social disabilities of Georgia behind them. The children achieve great success as Irish-Americans:

- James Augustine Healy became Bishop of Portland, Maine.

- Patrick Francis Healy became the rector then President of Georgetown University (1873-1881).

- Michael Morris Healy, Jr. joined the United States Revenue Cutter Service, becoming a celebrated sea captain, the sole representative of the U.S. government in the vast reaches of Alaska.

- Alexander Sherwood Healy also became a priest, director of the seminary in Troy, New York and rector of the Cathedral in Boston.

- Three sisters became nuns, one a Mother Superior.

Now, it must be emphasized that the Healy offspring were accepted as Irish American and "white" (whatever that means). The positions they obtained could not have been theirs if they had been black or even dark-skinned. Many other "white" people who knew about the Healys' mixed-race origins accepted them as Irish-Americans. Are the Healys therefore entitled to be counted among the ranks of Irish-Americans and included in Irish-American history?

Not according to "black" elites and their "white liberal" allies. Years after their deaths, the Healy family is being claimed as "black" because of their achievements. As in the case of Anatole Broyard, the late New York Times book critic and essayist, if they can't claim you when you're alive and fighting, the hyenas try to "kidnap" your memory after you're dead. James and Francis Healy have been betrayed by the Catholic Church they served so faithfully because insecure "black Catholics" want to claim "trophy" clergymen of high rank despite the fact that discrimination and lack of educational opportunities prevented real "blacks" from creating an impressive "resume" in the 19th century. James  Healy is now being described as the first "black" American to be ordained a priest and the first "black" bishop. Georgetown University now claims that Francis Patrick Healy (photo above) was the first "African American" president of a predominately "white" university and the first "black" to obtain a Ph.D. Some gratitude the Catholic Church has shown! It has insulted the memory of James and Francis Healy by effectively stating that they were not good enough for their Irish-American heritage but only fit to "improve" the "black race" with their "white blood." The Healys must be turning over in their graves!

Captain Michael Morris Healy's memory was recently tarnished by the United States Coast Guard, which named an  Icebreaker, the U.S.C.G.C. HEALY (launched in 1997) after him. Normally, it is a great honor to have a ship named after you. It is an insult, however, when the ship is named after you so the U.S. Coast Guard can honor a "black" hero who was really Irish-American, at least 3/4 white, and identified as both white and Irish. In this case, someone told a group of black schoolkids at Virgil Grissom Junior High School in Queens, New York that they had a "black" hero in Captain Healy. The black kids initiated a letter-writing campaign to get the Coast Guard to name a ship after Michael Healy. Now, these kids may be flattered by the idea that a person of obvious Caucasian phenotype shares their "race," but it is in fact a racial insult they are incapable of recognizing:

The Healy family's achievements do not show what "blacks" could do in the 19th century because they were NOT BLACK.

The overwhelmingly European ancestry of the Healy family does not "prove" the biological equality of "blacks." People will tacitly assume (as they always have) that "superior white blood" gave them their intelligence.

A prime example of the "liberal racism" that condemns the Healys as "black" on the basis of the "one drop" myth while pretending to be anti-racist and sympathetic, is "Racial Identity and the Case of Captain Michael Healy, USRCS," by James M. O'Toole, director of the archives program at University of Massachusetts, Boston. (*Quarterly of the National Archives & Records Administration*, Fall 1997, vol. 29, No. 3.)

O'Toole begins with a confrontation between Captain Healy and two sailors he was disciplining. He notes that they called him a "God damned Irishman." O'Toole is very upset that the sailors didn't call Captain Healy a "nigger." This seems to him the only natural thing to call Captain Healy. O'Toole throughout the article, projects his own racism and devotion to the "one drop" myth on 19th century Americans who obviously didn't share his devotion to white racial "purity."

O'Toole's racist devotion to the "one drop" myth blinds him to racial reality in the 19th century. He assumes that the "one drop" myth was law and universally accepted by "whites." It wasn't. Any research into racial classification laws in the 19th century would have shown him that various degrees of "negro blood" were accepted into the "white race," even in the Deep South. Also, the combination of a person's looks and the reputation he had established were all taken into consideration in determining whether one was "white" or not. It is obvious that Captain Healy and his siblings succeeded in establishing themselves as second-generation Irish Americans. O'Toole cannot bear this and insists that the Healy siblings were really "African Americans." He also calls their mother, Eliza, an "African American" even though her ancestry was at least half European.

O'Toole also claims that all "whites" believed in "mulatto inferiority" or the doctrine that mixed-race people are biologically inferior to BOTH or ALL "pure" parental groups. He is too ignorant to understand that this doctrine was created as a defense of slavery by pro-slavery intellectuals who wanted to counter the Northern anti-slavery argument that, if slavery is justified on the basis of "race," then "white" slaves should be automatically free because the negro racial "taint" had been effectively bred out of the line. Lawrence Tenzer explains the origins of this doctrine very well in his book *The Forgotten Cause of the Civil War: A New Look at the Slavery Issue*. O'Toole would do well to sit at Tenzer's feet and learn

something. O'Toole follows the usual liberal excuse of claiming that "society" defined the Healy family as "black," but ex-
presses wonderment at the fact that "whites" who knew about
Captain Healy's mixed ancestry still treated him as "white."
     O'Toole is amazed that establishing a "white" identity
was so easy for the Healys. "The apparent ease with which
they made the transition from black to white is striking." Hell,
any white-identified multiracial could have told him that!
First, they didn't start out as "black." All things would be
made clear if he would stop listening to and promoting
"black" propaganda. O'Toole is racist because he accepts the
myth that the Healys' real identity was "black" and that they
were only "passing" for white and Irish American. Even
though, like so many liberals, O'Toole acknowledges that
"Group boundaries are more fluid than we often suppose," he
clearly accepts and endorses the "one drop" myth, passing it
off as biological and social reality:

> Where the Healys are remembered today, it is as African Ameri-
> cans; several of them are now celebrated as the "first black"
> achievers in their fields. They themselves, however, recoiled
> from such an identification. Wherever possible, they sought a
> white identity...
>
> This may seem surprising or even disappointing to us...

     Why should it be "surprising" or "disappointing" to
anyone? The Healys embraced the identity that they believed
best defined them. The Irish American identity certainly described the Healys well—far better than any false "black"
identity. Does O'Toole really believe that the "white race" is
"pure" or totally free from the "taint" of the "race" in whose
equality he professes to believe? O'Toole also accepts the
"liberal" nonsense that a "white" identity is merely an attempt
to escape from "racism" and that the Healys would have
cheerfully accepted a "black" identity if there had been no
anti-black discrimination. Tell me, in a world free of anti-
Semitism, would Jews voluntary call themselves "non-
Aryans" or "kikes" or any other term invented to degrade
them? Of course not; the question would be considered ridiculous. Why, therefore, do liberal and "black" elites insist that,

in a prejudice-free world, people would cheerfully accept a racially degraded identity for themselves. Such idiocy constitutes a total rejection of logic.

Captain Healy married Mary Ann Roach, herself the daughter of Irish immigrants. O'Toole's racism keeps him still amazed that a "white" identity was passed on to their son:

> He repeatedly referred to white settlers [in Alaska] as "our people," and was even able to pass this racial identity on to a subsequent generation. His teenage son Fred, who accompanied his father on a voyage in 1883, scratched his name into a rock on a remote island above the Arctic Circle, proudly telling his diary that he was the first "white boy" to do so.

Imagine that! O'Toole can't understand how a boy with a white-identified Irish quadroon father and a "pure" Irish mother could presume to call himself "white" instead of some "black" nonsense. O'Toole appears to be really concerned about those polluting "black drops" contaminating his "whiteness." He apparently doesn't want to share his Irish American identity with people contaminated by the blood of the "race" he claims to champion.

O'Toole acknowledges that Captain Healy experienced prejudice for being Irish and Catholic, but he seems to be so disappointed that the "nigger" insult never pops up to put the uppity quadroon in his place. Indeed, O'Toole's liberal racist contention that the Healy family's Irish Catholic identity was mere social climbing to escape discrimination is even more ridiculous when you realize that, in the 19th century, both Irish and Catholics faced massive discrimination. If the Healys wanted to social climb, they could have become white Protestants.

The "racial kidnapping" of the Healy family is an important example of why the "liberal racist" assumption that a publicly-identified European heritage is somehow "too good" for those non-Hispanics "tainted" by "black blood" must be openly and defiantly challenged. We must end this racial "rape." If the Healy family can be violated in death, it can happen to anyone.

More "kidnapping" links:

(Please note that NONE of them, in listing the Healys as the first "black" this and that, bother to inform people that the Healys explicitly rejected that identification and called themselves both "white" and Irish-American.)

- <http://www.cviog.uga.edu/Projects/gainfo/tdgh-apr/apr06.htm> This Day in Georgia History, University of Georgia "blackens" James Augustine Healy.

- <http://gulib.lausun.georgetown.edu/dept/speccoll/c15 7.htm> Georgetown University – Rev. Patrick F. Healy, SJ Papers: Collection Description.

- <http://gulib.lausun.georgetown.edu/dept/speccoll/c15 7.htm> History and Background, October US Papal Visit. Church "blackens" Healy Brothers—admits they did not identify as such.

- <http://www.catholic.org/saints/black.html> "Black" Catholics organizations, shameless in their racial inferiority complex, are claiming James, Patrick and Alexander Healy as first "blacks" in terms of achievement within the Catholic Church, despite the fact that the Healys were not considered "black" and no real "black" could have obtained the positions they held.

IX. Racial Mixture, "White" Identity, and the "Forgotten" (or Censored) Cause of the Civil War
Originally published in *Interracial Voice* at
<http://www.interracialvoice.com/powell9.html>

Why would Northern whites oppose slavery while rejecting racial equality for blacks? This is a question one reads constantly in Civil War scholarship. However, the answer is obvious if one is willing to address taboo and "politically incorrect" subjects—"white" slavery and racial mixture. Obviously, the answer to this question also demands that historians acknowledge and deal with another forbidden subject—the definition of "white" and the impossibility of distinguishing the "mixed race white" from the "pure white." Equally taboo is dealing with the fact that, to most "whites," a fellow "white" is defined by looks and not racial "purity" or freedom from the dreaded "black blood." Now, how did this belief on the part of Northern "whites" contribute to the Civil War?

The Forgotten Cause of the Civil War: A New Look at the Slavery Issue by Lawrence R. Tenzer, Scholars Publishing House, 1997, shows how the whiteness of some slaves increased the fear and hatred of slavery in Northerners because of the possibility that any white person could be seized and taken South—especially after the passage of the Fugitive Slave Act of 1850. Tenzer states:

If "cause" can be defined as any political or social dynamic which exacerbated the tension between the North and South, then white slavery certainly qualifies because it contributed to the deep-rooted friction which existed between the free and slave sections of the country. Lincoln himself made references to slavery "regardless of color." The facts presented in this thoroughly researched text prove that white people were slaves in the American South and that white slavery was indeed a cause of the Civil War.

Tenzer is careful to define his terms. "The South" refers to the slavocracy—the political power that governed the slave states—not the Southern people in general. This definition embodies an important point. There were many poor and non-slaveholding whites throughout the Southern states who had no influence on proslavery politics. The oligarchy of Southern politicians and their slave holding allies were the power of the South, what came to be known as the "slave power." This is great. Tenzer puts the blame were it lies. Too many historians engage in lazy, meaningless and inaccurate racial generalizations such as "Whites decided that..." or "Whites believed..." Which "whites"? Indulging in collective guilt lets the guilty people off the hook

What Separates the "Mulatto" from the "White"? Can Slaves Be "White"? Can "Whites" Have "Negro Blood"?

The status of children born of white fathers and black or mulatto slave mothers was a pressing issue. The English Common Law said that a child follows the status of the father. However, that would mean that the issue of a female slave was not her master's property—in the way that the issue of female livestock were his property. In 1662 the Southern colony of Virginia was the first to pass legislation which attempted to regulate interracial fornication and marriage as well as the status of the mixed-blood children of slave mothers. Going back into classical Roman history, it confirmed the legal doctrine of *partus sequitur ventrem*, which held that the child follows the status of the mother. This early legal precedent had far reaching effects.

Tenzer emphasizes the fact that "negro blood" by itself did not make anyone a slave. It was the maternal descent of the *partus* rule that enslaved a person—if the maternal slave line was unbroken by legal manumission. A slaveholder could, legally, have more "negro blood" than his slave. A legal "white" man could have more Negro blood than a so-called "light mulatto" who would be legally "white" if he were manumitted. The latter was possible because the general Southern rule was to establish one-eighth or less Negro blood as the dividing line between "white" and "mulatto". Even this could be modified by such things as reputation, acceptance by the local "white" community, property ownership, etc. Hard as it may be for persons raised on "one drop" mythology to believe, a person classified as a "mulatto slave" would, if manumitted and one-eighth or less "black," legally become a free "white" person rather than a "free colored." As Thomas Jefferson, himself the reputed father of "white slaves," states:

> Our canon considers two crosses with the pure white, and a third with any degree of mixture, however small, as clearing the issue of the Negro blood. But observe, that this does not reestablish freedom, which depends on the condition of the mother, the principle of the civil law, *partus sequitur ventrem* being adopted here.

The South is caught in a major contradiction here. She has justified slavery on the basis of the alleged inferiority of the "negro race" but also implements the *partus* rule, while effectively enslaves people who are not only not "black" or "negro" but even "white."

If Slavery is Justified on the Basis of "Race," Shouldn't White Slaves Be Free? The Importance of White Slavery in Securing Support for the Abolitionist Cause

Many anti-slavery people argued that, if the South justified slavery on the basis of "race," then the loss of blackness justified a slave's freedom. This was a direct attack on the legal doctrine of *partus sequitur ventrem*. "White Slavery" was essentially a godsend for the abolitionist movement. It created an antipathy toward slavery that would not have been as widespread had all slaves been "black" or even dark-skinned. Moreover, with the uncomprehending assistance of the South herself, the movement was able to show white Northerners that they themselves were in personal danger from slavery. If the South would enslave its own "white" children, what wouldn't they do to the hated Yankees, "white" or not?

The term "white slave" was frequently used in 19th century abolitionist and Republican literature. There was also recognition that being "mixed race" and "white" were not mutually exclusive. The term "white mulatto" was frequently used to describe a combination of mixed racial descent and Caucasian phenotype. Anti-slavery activists encouraged novels and stories about "white slaves" in order to gain the empathy of Northern readers. The "tragic mulatto" stereotype has its origins in novels about "white slaves." Up through 1861, no less than 17 novels utilized a "white slave" theme. One of the most popular plays was *The Octoroon*. Indeed, it was scheduled to be performed at Ford's Theater in Washington, D.C. the day after Abraham Lincoln's assassination. The first anti-slavery novel, published in 1836, was about a white slave, *The Slave: or Memoirs of Archy Moore* by Richard Hildreth. After the passage of the 1850 Fugitive Slave Act, the novel's title was changed to *The White Slave: or, Memoirs of a Fugitive*. Harriet Beecher Stowe's *Uncle Tom's Cabin* (which Lincoln credited with helping to start the Civil War) utilized "white slave" characters. Furthermore, "Yankee" and foreign visitors who traveled to the South expecting to see black slavery were shocked and appalled whenever they saw slaves as white as any other "white." Indeed, this was usually the aspect of Southern life that left the greatest impression on them. If they talked or wrote about nothing else in Southern life, they took pains to mention the "perfectly white" slaves they saw in the slave states. Northern whites were being constantly exposed to this type of literature.

The "Slave Power" Responds: Slavery Is A Positive Good—and Not Dependent Upon Race or Color

The defenders of slavery reacted with the usual extremism, claiming that slavery was a good thing regardless of the race of the slaves, often pointing out the allegedly superior material conditions of Southern slaves to Northern laborers.

Indeed, abolitionists had only to quote Southern newspapers and political literature to make their point.

George Fitzhugh was one of the most important intellectual defenders of slavery. His *Sociology for the South, or the Failure of Free Society* (1854), was quoted extensively in the election campaign of 1856 and anti-slavery literature in general:

> Make the laboring man the slave of one man, instead of the slave of society, and he would be far better off.
>
> We do not adopt the theory that Ham was the ancestor of the negro race. The Jewish slaves were not negroes; and to confine the jurisdiction of slavery to that race would be to weaken its scriptural authority for we read of no negro slavery in ancient times. SLAVERY BLACK OR WHITE IS NECESSARY.

A South Carolina newspaper was widely quoted in abolitionist literature:

> The great evil of northern free society is that it is burdened with a servile class.... Slavery is the natural and normal condition of the laboring man, whether WHITE or black. The great evil of Northern free society is that it is burdened with a servile class of MECHANICS and LABOURERS, unfit for self government, yet clothed with the attributes and powers of citizens. Master and slave is a relation in society as necessary as that of parent and child; and the Northern States will yet have to introduce it. Their theory of free government is a delusion.

The *Richmond Enquirer* made the South's position plain:

> While it is far more obvious that negroes should be slaves than whites...yet the principle of slavery is itself right and does not depend on difference of complexion.

What could be clearer to Northerners? The South not only defended the principle that it is right to enslave people of any race or color, it proudly proclaimed its contempt for free labor, free society and the egalitarian principles of republicanism that most Northerners held sacred.

Would the Southern "Slave Power" Enslave Free Northern Whites? Why Northern Whites Had Reason to Fear the South

Anti-slavery activists were quick to point out that slavery endangered poor white Northern laborers. If Northerners were made slaves to Southern political power, then the next logical step would be the actual enslavement of free white people, especially those of the laboring class who were poor and vulnerable. Republican literature of the antebellum period constantly warns against "white slavery," and the South's barely hidden wish to eventually take over the entire country and expand the slave system to include Northern white laborers.

Many Northerners strongly believed that figurative white slavery would lead ultimately to literal white slavery for the free states. The proof of this was not only Southern political power at the federal level but the proved willingness of the Slave Power to put the sanctity of slave "property" above ties of race and kinship.

The abolitionist press played up the issue of white persons being kidnapped, and with good reason. The Fugitive Slave Law of 1850 provided for no protection against false identification. There was no formal hearing, no due process of any kind. The accused "slave" had no time to summon witnesses to vouch for his or her identity. In the case of a child claimed as a slave, this helplessness was even greater. Add to this the outrageous fact that the commissioner charged with determining the identity of the accused fugitive received double his fee if he found in favor of the slave-catcher. Bribery was built into the law. In response, Northern states passed a series of "personal liberty" laws to provide due process to accused slaves and nullify the effects of the federal law. Pro-slavery forces reacted with outrage to this assertion of "states' rights."

It is amazing to discover how much the issue of "white slaves" and "white slavery" were part of the antebellum political agenda. It is rarely mentioned today. Tenzer quotes from historian Russel B. Nye:

If slavery was a positive good, and the superior political, economic and social system that the South claimed it to be, it seemed reasonable to expect that the next step would be an attempt to impose it upon the nation at large for the nation's own good...It was easy, said the abolitionists, to take one more step, to show that if slavery were the best system for inferior races, it was also the best for inferior classes, regardless of race.

In 1858, Congressman Philemon Bliss of Ohio predicted the enslavement of free "white" labor if the South could not be checked:

> The more honest advocates of slavery have already repudiated the idea that it should be the sole condition of any race, and many of them would impose it upon all hand laborers. Free labor would have to compete with slave labor and could not survive.

Editorials like this one from the 1856 Marshall Statesman (Michigan) were common:

> The doctrine of white slavery is now openly broached South of the Potomac. This is no more than could be expected, because the difference in color, especially in Virginia, is so slight that sometimes it is absolutely impossible to tell whether an individual has any African blood in his veins or not.... hence rises this new doctrine... SLAVERY BLACK OR WHITE, IS RIGHT AND NECESSARY.

In 1856, *The Anti-Slavery Bugle* predicted the eventual enslavement of "white" immigrant labor:

> What security have the Germans and Irish that their children will not, within a hundred years, be reduced to slavery in this land of their adoption?...Is color any protection? No indeed.

It is relevant here to report an incident from another book, *Blood and Treasure: Confederate Empire in the Southwest* by Donald S. Frazier because it perfectly exemplifies the proslavery contempt for labor, free society and "social inferiors." In 1856, Philemon T. Herbert, a Democratic Congressman from Texas, shot and killed the Irish headwaiter at Willard's Hotel in Washington, D.C. for refusing to serve him breakfast after the posted time. This incident was widely publicized during that election year as evidence of Southern or proslavery contempt for all working people—white or otherwise. In the South itself, Herbert was hailed as a hero who acted exactly as a Southern gentleman should. He avenged an "insult" to his "honor" and put an "inferior" in his place. Add to this incident the even more infamous 1856 case of antislavery champion Senator Charles Sumner of Massachusetts being almost clubbed to death in the Senate chamber by South Carolina Congressman Preston S. Brooks (another matter of Southern "honor") and you can see how the North came to increasingly view the Southern "Slave Power" as fanatical and contemptuous of the rights of others—even "whites."

In 1862, *The Iron Platform*, a New York workingman's paper, knew what was really at stake during the Civil War.

> There is one truth which should be clearly understood by every workingman in the Union. The slavery of the black man leads to the slavery of the white man...If the doctrine of treason is true, that Capital should own labor, then their logical conclusion is correct, and all laborers, whether white or black, are and ought to be slaves.

Was the North Paranoid About White Slavery? Was the Threat to Northern Whites Real?

The North had good reason to fear the kidnapping of "whites" into slavery. The average "white" Southerner was quite poor. Hundreds of thousands of families lived on less than $100 per year. Even skilled laborers averaged no more than $600 or $700 a year. Consider then that the average price of a slave in 1850 was $400, more money than many ordinary people would earn in a year. The 1850s saw a rapid growth in slave prices, with many slaves being worth well over $1,000 or even $2,000. How many men would not be tempted to make a little kidnapping expedition to the North? And, if you found a person who looked like the "light mulatto" slave you were chasing, would you really care whether the suspect was indeed the fugitive or even a "pure" white when you have so much money to gain?

We must also consider the fact, that contrary to the neo-confederate view that the "War Between the States" was fought to free Southern states from the "tyranny" of the federal government, the antebellum period was characterized by Northern states asserting their rights and sovereignty against a proslavery federal tyranny. In addition to the 1850 Fugitive Slave Act, the North felt the power of the South and the tyranny of proslavery forces in these ways:

From 1836 to 1844 pro-slavery forces in the House of Representatives passed and implemented the so-called "gag rule," a nullification of the First Amendment right of free speech whereby antislavery petitions to Congress were no longer heard. From the 1830s until the Civil War, the Southern pro-slavery forces censored the United States mail. Postmasters were forbidden to deliver antislavery literature into the slave states. In 1845 Texas was annexed as a slave state. In 1846 the Wilmot Proviso, which would have banned slavery from the territories acquired in the Mexican-American War was defeated by proslavery forces in Congress. The Kansas-Nebraska Act of 1854 negated the Missouri Compromise and made slavery possible in any of the territories. New states that came from the territories could easily become slave states, thereby increasing Southern power. A proslavery U.S. Supreme Court existed from the 1840s until the Civil War.

Who could doubt that the South had the political power and will to eventually nationalize slavery and augment its slave population with the laboring classes of the free states?

The Theory of Mulatto Inferiority: The Slave Power's Answer to the Charge of White Slavery

The abolitionists' challenge to the "Slave Power" regarding "white slavery" had to be answered. It was answered with the theory of "mulatto" inferiority." This is not the racist belief with which most of us are familiar - the idea that mixed-race people are "superior" to the "pure black" but "inferior" to the "pure white" depending upon the degree of "white blood." No, this theory's racism was infinitely greater. It was based upon the assumption that "whites" and "blacks" are like two different species and their mixed-race offspring

were sterile, degenerate, and inferior to both parental "races."
What made the "mulatto" and mixed "white" far more threat-
ening to slavery than the "black," was the higher regard in
which they were held by "whites" in general. Indeed, Tenzer
notes that from the late 1700s onward, many observations
were made about mulattoes being very physically attractive
and intelligent. Here are just two of several such quotes from
The Forgotten Cause of the Civil War:

English traveler Edward S. Abdy, 1835 recalled:

... the dread that the species will be deteriorated by "crossing the
breed"; though every one knows, who is capable of comparing
forms and figures, that the finest specimens of beauty and sym-
metry are to be found among those whose veins are filled with
mixed blood.

Dr. Benjamin Rush, a signer of the Declaration of Independence, said in 1811:

It is possible, the strength of the intellects may be improved in
their original conformation, as much as the strength of the body,
by certain mixtures of persons of different nations, habits, and
constitutions, in marriage. The mulatto has been remarked, in all
countries, to exceed in sagacity, his white and black parent.

Tenzer notes that historian Robert Brent Toplin researched the attitudes of whites toward mulattoes in the South
during the period from 1830 to 1861. He has concluded that in
addition to often being thought of as physically attractive and
intelligent, they were frequently taught skills and given extraordinary responsibilities. Note that while it was considered
a great insult to call a "white" person a "mulatto" (Many
"whites" sued in court and won large judgments against people who called them "mulatto" or challenged their legal standing as "whites"), there was still a common belief that the mulatto was very much like the "white,"—especially if he or she
"looked white."

Many influential people such as Senator Henry Clay
of Kentucky, proslavery writer William Gilmore Simms and
Congressman James M. Ashley of Ohio believed that the
"black race" was destined, through amalgamation, to eventually disappear into the "white race."

The proslavery intellectuals had to counteract these positive attitudes. Tenzer describes their dilemma very well. In order to keep the institution of slavery intact and not allow any part of it to be compromised, the South had to find a way to defend the enslavement of all mulattoes, regardless of the degree of admixture. This was done with theories that attacked the idea that mulattoes were approaching conformity with whites.

The father of the theory of "mulatto inferiority" was Dr. Josiah Clark Nott of Mobile, Alabama. His theory was first published in 1843 in an article for the *American Journal of the Medical Sciences* entitled "The Mulatto a Hybrid - probable extermination of the two races if the Whites and Blacks are allowed to intermarry." A reprint appeared shortly after in the *Boston Medical and Surgical Journal*. He introduced the theory of "mulatto sterility" into the "scientific" community, and his theory was quoted by "anti-miscegenation" judges and lawmakers until the end of the Jim Crow era.

One may ask how anyone could believe such a preposterous "scientific theory," since anybody who lived near mulattoes could see that they reproduced just as well as "whites" or "blacks." Tenzer explains:

> Of course mulattoes produced children like everyone else, so the sterility theory incorporated the idea that fertility deteriorated through subsequent generations with sterility being the inevitable end. Nott conceived of mulattoes as having weak and frail constitutions, high mortality, and infertility. The more white admixture mulattoes had, the greater their physical problems. According to Nott's theories, light mulattoes could never approach being white because blacks and whites were two different species...

In other words, Nott claimed that this alleged degeneration and infertility only occurred with white intermixture. He had no objection to these "hybrids" mating with blacks, nor did he concern himself with any of this alleged infertility in mulatto/black matings. Nott's purpose was to defend slavery by denying the abolitionists' contention that white people were being enslaved:

It has been asserted by writers, that when the grade of Quinteroon [one-sixteenth black—a cross between a white and an octoroon] is arrived at, all trace of black blood is lost, and that they cannot be distinguished from the whites. Now if this be true, most of the Mulattoes must cease to breed before they arrive at this point of mixture; for though I have passed most of my life in places where the two races have been mingling for many generations, I have rarely if ever met an individual tainted with black blood, in whom I could not detect it without difficulty. These higher grades should be extremely common if the chain were not broken by death and sterility. How else can the fact be accounted for?

The obvious answer is that the offspring of the "higher grades" were socially and legally integrated into the "white race." Remember that while Nott is writing this idiotic "theory," the laws of most Southern states allowed people with more "black blood" than a "quinteroon" to become legal "whites." This was, of course, a silent process not boasted of in Southern writing. But, since there was still a stigma attached to publicly acknowledging "black" ancestry, these "whites" would not identify themselves as being of mixed ancestry or protest this new stigma. Thus, Nott and his ideological confederates were free to publicize their lies without the "proof" of their nonsense being presented to the public.

Tenzer also relates how the 1840 U.S. Census was used as "proof" of mulatto "inferiority" by the creation of bogus "insanity" rates in the predominately mulatto "free colored" population compared to the slave population. The "sterility theory" was "supported" by pointing out the supposedly higher fertility of slaves compared to free mulattoes, totally ignoring factors such as the illegal slave trade from Cuba and Africa, the kidnapping of free people into slavery, and the deliberate breeding of slaves. These factors bore the primary responsibility, in that order, of augmenting slaves numbers beyond a natural rate of increase. We might also add that free people often have schooling, work or travel ambitions that cause them to postpone starting families. Slaves would generally have no reason to postpone reproduction and would be actively discouraged from doing so by their owners.

Tenzer reminds us that, ridiculous as Nott's ideas were, they were perpetuated by men who were educated and sophisticated in promoting racist doctrines. When a theory of "mulatto inferiority" appears in the "best" of the "scientific" journals, who is an "uneducated" lay person to question it? "Science" was effectively used in the service of politics and the defense of slavery. Tenzer effectively summarizes the hypocrisy here:

According to Southern laws, those who were free and less than one-fourth or one-eighth black were legally defined as white people; those who were slaves and had any admixture of white and black blood whatsoever were physiologically considered frail and sterile hybrids...who were subject to insanity if freed from slavery.

The refusal to admit that "Negro blood" was and is entering the "white race" is still a tacit understanding among both Southern and Northern elites. It is a small wonder that the "white slavery" issue is rarely addressed in modern history classes and academic literature.

Conclusion

The Forgotten Cause of the Civil War inspires us to ask questions that most American historians are afraid to ask:

Would the Civil War have occurred if the existence of "white slaves" had not brought home to Northern citizens the great danger that slavery posed to a free society?

Why are racial mixture and mixed-race people relegated to the margins of American history when knowledge of their origins and legal status are essential to understanding the tensions between North and South that led to the Civil War?

Why is the anti-slavery movement presented to modern students as merely an altruistic concern for "blacks," with no mention made of the threat to all poor and working class "whites" and "free society" in general?

If slaves could be "white," and legal "whites" could be partially "black," are they not part of "white" or European American history and populations and not just some "exotic" variety of "African Americans"?

It is no accident that *The Forgotten Cause of the Civil War* has not received the attention it deserves. The lack of respect for "mixed race" history within American history reflects the lack of respect for, and recognition of, mixed-race people in general. The Civil War is one of the most popular subjects in American society. It is time for us to remind Americans of its "forgotten" cause.

Epilogue

The follow-up below was originally published in *Interracial Voice* as URL
<http://www.interracialvoice.com/powell12.html>

"White Slavery" means the enslavement, in the ante-bellum South, of people who were physically "white." "White slaves" were presumed to be descended from a "black" female slave according to the maternal descent rule of inherited slave status. There was no way to really determine who was descended from a female African slave and who was "pure" white. If the slave descent was broken by manumission, "white" slaves could often become legally "white." Northerners, who were told by the Southern slaveholding elite that slavery was justified by the "inferiority" of the "black race," were horrified to discover that people as white as themselves were being held as slaves. Southern political power and the federal Fugitive Slave Law allowed slave catchers to seize alleged fugitives from bondage with no due process. "White slavery" meant that one's physical appearance was no protection from legal kidnapping. The political ramifications of this fact, unacknowledged by most American historians, are that anti-slavery politics increasingly emphasized the threat of slavery to Northern whites. The fear and hatred of slavery was usually not, as commonly believed, an altruistic response to the sufferings of "blacks" by liberal "whites." Racial intermixture and mixed-race "whites" were, therefore, important factors in increasing the tensions that ultimately led to the American Civil War, and not just marginal characters in bad melodramas.

To *Interracial Voice* Readers from A.D. Powell:

This is a crusade for justice. The issue of "white slavery" in the antebellum South has FINALLY received some recognition in academic circles. "White Slavery: An American Paradox" by Carol Wilson and Calvin D Wilson in *Slavery and Abolition*, 19:1. "The Slave Trader, the White Slave, and the Politics of Racial Determination in the 1850s" by Walter Johnson in *Journal of American History*, 87:1, (June 2000).

However, the definitive work on "white" chattel slavery and its political ramifications—Lawrence R. Tenzer's *The Forgotten Cause of the Civil War: A New Look at the Slavery Issue* (Manahawkin, NJ: Scholars' Publishing House, 1997)—has not been reviewed in any academic journal or even cited in a scholarly bibliography. Any idiot who wants to write fairy tales about mythological "black" Confederate soldiers bravely defending their Southern homeland from the marauding Yankees can find a publisher, but Dr. Tenzer's 21 years of research in PRIMARY documents has been rejected by publishers. Why? Consider these possible reasons:

The Forgotten Cause answers a question that American historians are always asking but don't really want answered: Why was slavery the great moral and political issue of the antebellum period if it affected only "blacks," a people who were deemed an "inferior race"? If slavery was a threat to "whites" in general, and "white slaves" were recognized as fellow "whites" by Northerners, historians must admit that there was no clear dividing line between the "races." They must acknowledge that Southern slavery was a threat to Americans in general. Neither "liberal" nor "conservative" historians want to admit that.

Neo-Confederate historians constantly argue in the popular press that the Confederacy fought, not for slavery, but for "states' rights" and against some kind of federal tyranny. Tenzer shows that it was Northern states who exercised their "states' rights" by passing personal liberty laws to nullify the effects of the federal Fugitive Slave Law. This law gave the accused slave, who could be "white," no right to bring witnesses, have a jury, or any other forms of due process. The

judge was authorized by the law to receive a larger fee if he
ruled against the accused slave than if he ruled in his or her
favor. Why do "liberal" historians refuse to publicize these
facts when they totally devastate the Neo-Confederate nonsense about an abstract devotion to "states' rights"?

Other academics, such as Werner Sollors, have noted
that abolitionist literature constantly emphasized white slavery. It's hard to find an abolitionist novel that doesn't feature
quadroons, octoroons, etc. If slavery was justified by "race,"
shouldn't a "white" slave be free? Tenzer unearths the pro-
slavery apologists who seriously argued that SLAVERY
WHITE OR BLACK was justified and the institution didn't
need an "inferior race" to justify its existence. If historians acknowledge that the South's intellectual defenders were willing
to promote slavery as superior to free society and openly suggest that poor Northern laborers would be better off as property, what happens to the South's glorious "Lost Cause"?
What happens to the useless arguments about how much
Northern "whites" liked or disliked "blacks," or the Neo-
Confederate nonsense that the presence of "black" (actually,
wealthy mulatto) slaveholders "proves" that slavery was not
the cause of the war?

Finally, Tenzer researched antebellum Republican political literature to show that the threat of "white slavery" was
used by Abraham Lincoln's party to galvanize voters. The Republican Party activists, Lincoln included, knew that Northerners had good reason to fear the South and its insatiable
need for more and more slaves. Southern pro-slavery apologists constantly stated that their slaves were better off than
free white laborers in the North. More than that, the pro-
slavery intellectuals defended slavery as a good in and of itself, regardless of "race" or "color." While the current fashion
is to argue that Southern states were merely resisting the tyranny of a federal government, we forget that The South effectively controlled Congress and the Presidency for most of the
antebellum period. Northern whites had seen the Fugitive
Slave Act shoved down their throats, the mails censored, and
the expansion of slavery into new territories. Abraham Lin-

coln wasn't the only one who knew that the nation couldn't exist half slave and half free - it would become ALL SLAVE or all free. If slave society had triumphed over free society, who is naive enough to think that greedy slave owners wouldn't have used their power to add many poor whites and Indians to their human property? Once we acknowledge these facts, what happens to the cherished myths of both liberal and Neo-Confederate historians?

Interracial Voice readers, if you have ANY contacts in publishing, the history profession, the media, etc., please promote *The Forgotten Cause*. University students, introduce the book to your professors and fellow students. People who are NOT "gatekeepers" of information seem to have no trouble understanding Dr. Tenzer's thesis. Only those with POWER suddenly lose their reading comprehension. If only ONE of them breaks ranks, it could make all the difference in the world.

X. Are "White" Americans All "Passing as White"?
The Alchemy of "Race"

Originally published in *Interracial Voice* at
<http://www.interracialvoice.com/powell11.html>

Whiteness of a Different Color: European Immigrants and the Alchemy of Race by Matthew Frye Jacobson. Harvard University Press, 1998.

Hardly two [scientists] agree as to the number and composition of the races. Thus one scholar makes an elaborate classification of twenty-nine races; another tells us there are six; Huxley gives us four; Kroeber three; Goldenweiser, five; and Boas inclines to two, while his colleague, Linton, says there are twelve or fifteen. Even my dullest students sometimes note this apparent contradiction. — Brewton Berry, "A Southerner Learns about Race," *Common Ground* (1942)

Matthew Frye Jacobson's *Whiteness of a Different Color* tells us all how we got in this mess. The book is subtitled *European Immigrants and the Alchemy of Race*. "Alchemy" is correct. It means that the "base metal" of Nordic, Alpine, Mediterranean and even Western Asian "races" were turned into the "gold" of unadulterated white status. Jacobson explains how "whiteness" was created by colonial elites for the purpose of defending the state from Indian invasions and slave insurrections, and continued by the American republic in order to create a sense of unity in its polyglot European immigrant population. In 1790, United States naturalization law granted citizenship to "free white persons"—which meant, mostly, those of Anglo-Saxon descent. As the U.S. population became more culturally mixed beginning in the 1840s, with an increase in immigration from non-Anglo Europe, the nation experienced "a fracturing of whiteness into a hierarchy of plural and scientifically determined white races."

In other words, people who came from Ireland, Poland, Germany, Italy, Greece, and Jews from Russia and other Slavic nations all became, by virtue of the "melting pot" ethic, "Caucasian" whites. But, the creation of whiteness was - and still is - by no means an easy, continuous process. The Celtic, Nordic, Alpine and Mediterranean "races" were abolished in favor of the myth of one homogenous "white" race (with the adoption of the "scientific" term "Caucasian" providing a new legitimacy to the honorific "racial" term "white."

Jacobson contends that traditional historians have deliberately dismissed the "racial" distinctions of the 19th century and before as "misuses" of the word "race." Of course they didn't mean that Irish, Germans, Bohemians, Nordics, etc. were separate races; they just didn't know what they were saying. This is a courtesy not given to mulattoes. Jacobson, however, shows that there was no "misuse." "Patterns in literary, legal, political and graphic evidence" show that the perception of race was very different from the standard rhetoric promoted in today's U.S. I have a sense of deja vu here. As I stated in a review of Lawrence R. Tenzer's The Forgotten Cause of the Civil War, mainstream historians' inability to acknowledge the fact that 19th century Northern "whites" saw predominately European slaves as "white," makes them deliberately blind to the role "white slavery" played as a cause of the Civil War. Few historians wish to deal with the fact that, while "white" privilege in various forms has been a constant in American political culture since colonial times, whiteness itself has been subject to all kinds of contests and has gone through a series of historical vicissitudes.

Jacobson divides the history of whiteness in the United States into three great epochs:

The nation's first naturalization law in 1790 (limited naturalized citizenship to "free white persons") demonstrates the republican convergence of race and "fitness for self-government"; the law's wording denotes an unconflicted view of the presumed character and unambiguous boundaries of whiteness.

Fifty years later, however, beginning with the massive influx of highly undesirable but nonetheless "white" persons from Ireland, whiteness was subject to new interpretations. The period of mass European immigration, from the 1840s to the restrictive legislation of 1924, witnessed a fracturing of whiteness into a hierarchy of plural and scientifically determined white races. Vigorous debate ensued over which of these was truly "fit for self-government" in the old Anglo-Saxon sense.

Finally, in the 1920s and after, partly because the crisis of over-inclusive whiteness had been solved by restrictive legislation and partly in response to a new racial alchemy generated by African-American migrations to the North and West, whiteness was reconsolidated: the late nineteenth century's probationary white groups were now remade and granted the scientific stamp of authenticity as the unitary Caucasian race - an earlier era's Celts, Slavs, Hebrews, Iberics, and Saracens, among others, had become Caucasians so familiar to our own visual economy and racial lexicon.

Before we learn how Europeans became "whites" and "whites" became "Caucasians," we should know the origin of "Caucasian."

The Most Beautiful "Race" in the World? A Georgian Skull and the Origin of the "Caucasian Race"

Caucasian Variety. I have taken the name of this variety from Mount Caucasus, both because its neighborhood, and especially the southern slope, produces the most beautiful race of men, I mean the Georgian;... That stock displays...the most beautiful form of the skull, from which, as from a mean and primeval type, the others diverge... Besides, it is white in color, which we may fairly assume to be the primitive color of mankind, since... it is very easy to degenerate into brown, but very much more difficult for dark to become white. — Johann Friedrich Blumenbach, On the Natural Varieties of Mankind (1775).

Of all the odd myths that have arisen in the scientific world, the "Caucasian mystery" invented quite innocently by Blumenbach is the oddest. A Georgian woman's skull was the handsomest in his collection. Hence it became his model exemplar of human skulls, from which all others might be regarded as deviations; and out of this, by some strange intellectual hocus-pocus, grew up the notion that the Caucasian man is the prototypic "Adamic" man. —
Thomas Henry Huxley, Methods and Results of Ethnology (1868)

Johann Friedrich Blumenbach (1752-1840), one of the founders of modern anthropology, ranked "races" on the basis of aesthetic judgment. He thought that the Georgians, a people who are native to the Caucasus mountain region, were the most "beautiful" people in the world. The "beauty" of each "race" was ranked by how close each one came to an "ideal" skull that Blumenbach found in Georgia. He therefore assumed that "whites" in general originated in the Caucasus because "white" features were closest to Blumenbach's aesthetic ideal. Because of Blumenbach's obsession with Georgian "beauty," the word "Caucasian" became a "scientific" synonym for "white." However, Blumenbach's ranking was based more on facial features as opposed to skin color. This is why anthropology texts have usually claimed that "Caucasian" skin color can range from the fairest Swede to nearly "black" natives of India - as long as the features are sharp, the eyes "round," and the hair is straight, wavy or curly.

This idea that "Caucasians" are the "beautiful race" beside whom all others fall short has never gone away. We see it on TV and the movies, where obviously multiracial women of "tan Caucasian" phenotypes are chosen as sex symbols for "black" males. Marriage advertisements placed by Hindus and Muslims from the Indian sub-continent and the Middle East are not shy about demanding "fair" brides (not as necessary for bridegrooms). Mexican and other Latin American television and film industries use "white" faces in front of the camera because darker ones are considered lacking in attractiveness.

Understanding Probationary and Contested Whiteness

Who is "white" and are there degrees of "whiteness"? Jacobson provides the following case as a major example of the ambiguity of this question:

> *In Rollins v. Alabama* (1922), an Alabama Circuit Court of Appeals reversed the conviction of one Jim Rollins, a black man convicted of the crime of miscegenation, on the grounds that the state had produced "no competent evidence to show that the woman in question, Edith Labue was a white woman." Labue was a Sicilian immigrant, a fact that, this court held, "can in no sense be taken as conclusive that she was therefore a white woman, or that she was not a negro or a descendant of a negro." Although it is important to underscore that this court did not find that a Sicilian was necessarily nonwhite, its finding that a Sicilian was inconclusively white does speak volumes about whiteness in 1920s Alabama. If the court left room for the possibility that Edith Labue may have been white, the ruling also made clear that she was not the sort of white woman whose purity was to be "protected" by that bulwark of white supremacism, the miscegenation statute.

This ruling is not an oddity of the Alabama courts, but part of a much broader pattern of racial thinking throughout the United States between the mid-nineteenth century and the mid-twentieth. ...In his 1908 study Race or Mongrel? Alfred Schultz lamented in unambiguously biological language:

> The opinion is advanced that the public schools change the children of all races into Americans. Put a Scandinavian, a German, and a Magyar boy in at one end, and they will come out Americans at the other end. Which is like saying, let a pointer, a setter, and a pug enter one end of a tunnel and they will come out three greyhounds at the other end.

Jacobson points out that in her 1910 study of Homestead, Pennsylvania, the sociologist Margaret Byington broke the community down along the "racial" lines of "Slav, English-speaking European," native, white, and colored." H.L. Mencken later casually alluded to the volume of literature crossing his desk by "Negro and other non-Nordic writers." When Porgy and Bess appeared (1935) critics broadly attributed George Gershwin's talent for "American-Negroid music" to the "common Oriental ancestry in both Negro and Jew." In other words, not all Americans saw the social divisions of the nation as simply "white" versus "black."

We must cease to think of contested whiteness as something from *Imitation of Life* and other works obsessed with "Negro blood" in otherwise "white" persons. Most of the officially "pure white" population is descended from people who were, at one time, not considered truly "white." They were on "probation," eventually graduating to full whiteness in a long and untidy process. As Jacobson explains it:

> The boundary over whiteness—its definition, its internal hierarchies, its proper boundaries, and its rightful claimants has been critical to American culture throughout the nation's history, and it has been a fairly untidy affair. Conflicting or overlapping racial designations such as 'white," "Caucasian," and "Celt" may operate in popular perception and discussion simultaneously, despite their contradictions—the Irish simians of the Thomas Nast cartoon, for example, were "white" according to naturalization law; they proclaimed themselves "Caucasians" in various political organizations using that term; and they were degraded "Celts" in the patrician lexicon of proud Anglo-Saxons. Indeed, this is the nature of ideological contest. Such usages have had regional valences as well: it is one of the compelling circumstances of American cultural history that an Irish immigrant in 1877 could be a despised Celt in Boston—a threat to the republic—and yet a solid member of The Order of Caucasians for the Extermination of the Chinaman in San Francisco, gallantly defending U.S. shores from an invasion of "Mongolians."

How did the honorific "racial" term "white" originate? Would you believe it was related to the need for a militia?

"Free White Persons" in the Republic 1790-1840 or We Need Somebody to Fight Off Those Slaves and Indians

The Third Charter of Virginia (1611-1612) dedicates the colony to "the propagation of the Christian Religion, and Reclaiming of People barbarous, to Civility and Humanity."

The Declaration of Proposals of the Lord Proprietor of Carolina (1663), the Charter of Rhode Island and Providence Plantations (1663) all defined the mission of their colonies as the taking of land from "barbarous" natives and their conversion to Christianity and a European (specifically English) way of life.

These colonial documents do not use the word "white," Jacobson says, but between the charters of the early seventeenth century and the naturalization law of the late eighteenth, the word "white" did attain wide usage in New World political discourse, and it was written into an immense body of statutory law. In the colonies the designation "white" appeared in laws governing who could marry whom, who could participate in the militia; who could vote or hold office; and in laws governing contracts, indenture and enslavement. The term "white" was used to confer rights and freedoms (except limiting one's right to marry). Citizenship became inseparable from the idea of whiteness and maleness because a citizen's primary duty was to help put down slave rebellions and participate in wars against the Indians. In other words, colonial British elites first created "white people" as a social and political category to create a sense of European solidarity against slaves and Indian nations. The colonial European population, divided by class, religion and national origin, had to be united. People who had little land and no slaves themselves had to be made to feel a certain brotherhood with large landowners and slave holders. It is no accident that Congress established a Uniform Militia (1792) defined as "each and every free able-bodied white male citizen of the respective states." In return for this military obligation, "white" men received the franchise (with property qualifications), the right to hold office and other rights superior to women and non-white males.

Another important component of political whiteness was Republican ideology. If the Crown of England was no longer the ruler, and the Revolution had been fought in the name of self-rule or rule by "the people"—the majority—then who were these citizens and what determined their fitness to rule? Furthermore, the Revolution's ideals meant different things to different classes. A planter aristocrat like George Washington or Thomas Jefferson did not necessarily want the kind of political equality favored by a New England farmer or a small merchant or artisan. The new American ruling class was thus presented with a dilemma—how to rule without overtly appearing to do so. In the Enlightenment's model of race and politics, the ideal republic was ruled by men who were logical, balanced and not given to irrational passions. Non-white "races" were, by definition, the opposite of this ideal, and most European "races" were judged inferior to the English—the standard by which all other "races" would be judged. The polity should be "a homogenous body" whose interests were, when thoughtfully considered, one and the same. The ideal American citizen's concept of "the public good" should be, essentially, the good of wealthy planters and merchants.

Massive Immigration, 1840-1924, and a Crisis of Whiteness

The Irish Famine Migration of the 1840s produced the first true crisis of whiteness in the American republic, according to Jacobson. Whereas the salient feature of whiteness before the 1840s had been its powerful political and cultural contrast to nonwhites, especially Indians and Africans and mixed- race Americans, this period is characterized by:

- A spectacular rate of American industrialization, whose voracious appetite for cheap labor encouraged hordes of non-English Europeans to come to the United States.

- A growing nativist perception of these laborers as a political threat to the smooth functioning of the republic.

- Consequently, a fracturing of monolithic whiteness by the popular marriage of scientific doctrines of race with political concerns over the newcomers' "fitness for self-government."

Why a threat? The demographics of the republic began to change dramatically in the 1840s. Consider these figures:

- 1820 - 8,385 immigrants from all sending countries
  combined

- 1847 (worst year of the Irish Famine) - 234,968 immigrants, of whom nearly half were from Ireland

- From 1846 to 1855 - a total of 3,031,339 immigrants,
  including 1,288,307 from Ireland and 976,711 from
  Germany, the two leading sources of immigration in
  this period.

- Combined with Italians, Russian Jews and other
  Europeans, the "white" foreign-born population of the
  U.S. reached 13.5 million by 1920.

We have to understand the tremendous changes and
fear created by this massive immigration and why these
"white" immigrants were in a state of probationary or contested "whiteness."

Are the Irish White?

In *The Inequality of Human Races* (1855) Arthur
Comte de Gobineau predicted the decline of the Anglo-Saxons
in America, now overwhelmed by the most degenerate races
of olden day Europe. They are the flotsam of all ages: Irish,
cross-bred German and French, and Italians of even more
doubtful stock.

Negative assessments of the Irish character are rooted
in the history of English conquest and hostility toward Ca-
tholicism. (An outlawed religion for much of English history.)
They were "savages" to be tamed, similar to Indians. They
had fine land that they supposedly didn't deserve or know
how to use properly.

Jacobson even shows us that 19th century Americans
had perceptions of distinctive Celtic physical characteristics.
Harper's Weekly (1851) described "the Celtic physiognomy"
as, among other things, "the small and somewhat upturned

nose [and] the black tint of the skin." While this opinion
sounds incredible to us, we must remember that a "racial" label often causes people to "see" differences that are not there.
Many people, both Irish and non-Irish, thought they saw distinctive Celtic physical types. Here's an opinion of Irish mor-
als and intelligence:

> *Atlantic Monthly* (1896): A Celt lacks the solidity, the balance,
> the judgement [sic], the moral staying power of the Anglo-
> Saxon." The Celt "imbibes with avidity the theory of equality,
> and with true Celtic ardor pushes it to excess; there are many
> Irish-Americans, young men growing up in our cities, who are
> too vain or too lazy to work, self-indulgent, impudent, and dissi-
> pated.

Irish were often compared unfavorably to "Negroes":
The Atlantic Monthly (1864): The emancipated Negro
is at least as industrious and thrifty as the Celt, takes more
pride in self-support, is far more eager for education, and has
fewer vices.

A famous political cartoon of 1876 shows the "Celt"
and the "Negro" on the scales of civic virtue and finds them
weighing in identically—an argument that seems to favor
stripping the Celt of official "white" status rather than raising
the "Negro" up.

It is ironic that the predominately Celtic and racially
mixed Healy Family—which produced Alaskan hero Captain
Michael Healy as well as James Healy, Bishop of Portland,
Maine and Patrick Healy, President of Georgetown University—is today denounced by "blacks" and "white" liberals as
"passing for white" social climbers for embracing their Irish
ancestry and identity instead of submitting to a "black"
stigma. If you were social climbing in 19th century America,
you would not want to be either Irish or Catholic and certainly
not both.

Are Italians White?

In *Rollins v. Alabama* (1922), as we have seen, a Si-
cilian woman was not deemed "white" enough by an Alabama
court to legally prevent a "black" man from mating with her.

Italians in Louisiana were also deemed unworthy of full "whiteness" and its privileges.

Many Italians are quite swarthy, olive or even brown-skinned. This is not surprising, given Italy's geographical closeness to Africa. In 1891 a "white" Louisiana mob lynched 11 Italians, What made Italians non-white in their eyes despite their immigration to the U.S. as "free white persons"? Jacobson says that Italians did not "act white" by Southern standards. They socialized freely with "blacks" and worked at "black" jobs. They also supported Republican and Populist political candidates. Were many of these "blacks" in fact mixed-race Creoles? Physically, Italians and Creoles are very similar. Culturally, they are both Roman Catholic and "Latin." Since Jacobson says that Italians intermarried with "blacks," these mates were probably not "black" at all but Creole.

Are Jews White?

Anyone who believes that Jewish people have always been considered "white" is ignorant of Jewish history—both medieval and modern. The Holocaust was a genocide directed against Jews and others that the Third Reich deemed "inferior races" who threatened the "purity" of "superior" German or "Aryan" blood. Sound familiar? Jacobson devotes an entire chapter, "Looking Jewish, Seeing Jews," to the ambiguous "racial" position of Jews in the United States. It was quite common, until the mid-twentieth century, for the media to refer to Jews in "racial" terms:

In *Types of Mankind* (1855) Josiah Nott remarked that the "well-marked Israelitish features are never beheld out of that race"; the complexion may be bleached or tanned... but the Jewish features stand unalterably through all climates."

The most dramatic example of Jews' racial ambiguity was the infamous Leo Frank case (1915), in which a "white" Jewish man in Georgia was convicted of murdering a working-class white girl—all on the testimony of a "Negro" janitor named Jim Conley. In the South at that time, it was considered culturally impossible for a "white" man to be convicted of anything on the word of a "Negro." Frank was sentenced to death on the word of a "Negro" of poor reputation and who was, logically, the most likely murder suspect. Reporters, both "white" and "Negro," questioned Frank's "racial" classification. He was officially, on paper, a "white" man, yet he was being treated more like a "Negro." Jacobson maintains that Frank's conviction was a sign of his contested whiteness. Frank was inconclusively white and therefore, by Southern standards, did not deserve the "respect" normally due "white" men. When the governor of Georgia commuted Frank's death sentence, Leo Frank was lynched by a "white" mob—a stereotypical "Negro" fate.

Moving up into the later 20th century, American Jewish writer Philip Roth shows that the possibility of losing "whiteness" is still in the mind of American Jews. Jacobson gives us this extensive quote from Roth's *Counterlife* (1988), in which a Gentile woman chances to comment that she seldom repays the attention of Jewish men "because there are enough politics in sex without racial politics coming into it." "We're not a race," objects her Jewish listener. The ensuing exchange cuts to the very heart of "difference" and the epistemology of race.

"It is a racial matter," she insisted.

"No, we're the same race. You're thinking of Eskimos."

"We are not the same race. Not according to anthropologists, or whoever measures these things. There's Caucasian, Semitic - there are about five different groups. Don't look at me like that."

"I can't help it. Some nasty superstitions always tend to crop up when people talk about a Jewish 'race.'"

"... All I can tell you is that you are a different race. We're supposed to be closer to Indians than to Jews, actually; - I'm talking about Caucasians."

"But I am a Caucasian, kiddo. In the U.S. census I am, for good or bad, counted as Caucasian."

"Are you? Am I wrong?"

This conversation should not be surprising given the history of Jewish persecution by Europeans. Even today, Jews are at the heart of right-wing racial ideology, defined as racially mixed or plotting the "mongrelization" of the "white race."

Jacobson summarizes the American Jewish "racial" situation very well:

> Across the latter half of the nineteenth century Jews, by common consensus, did represent a distinct race; but by the mid-twentieth such certainties had evaporated... the racial odyssey of American Jews from "white persons" to "Hebrews" to "Caucasians" illustrate how historical circumstance, politically driven categorization, and the eye of the beholder all conspire to create distinctions of race that are nonetheless experienced as natural phenomena, above history and beyond question.

Eugenics and the *Passing of the Great Race*

The Immigration Act of 1924 gave precedence to immigrants from Northern Europe and was designed to make sure that the U.S. would never again be deluged with "undesirable" immigrants, especially those from Southern and Eastern Europe. Jews, especially, were targets of the new immigration law. It is no accident that the 1924 Immigration Act occurs in the same year as Virginia's "Racial Integrity" Act of 1924—which banned non-Caucasian blood from the "white race." The eugenics movement was the ideological midwife of both laws. (For an example of how this era affected Americans of racially-mixed descent, see the Melungeon Homepage.) Jacobson places great emphasis on Madison Grant's *The Passing of the Great Race* as the "Mein Kampf" of the eugenics movement:

> Among the most important and popular expressions of the rising eugenic view of immigration was Madison Grant's *The Passing of the Great Race*, an extended diatribe against the "pathetic and fatuous belief in the efficacy of American institutions" to absorb and transform diverse populations. The book first appeared in 1916, but achieved its peak popularity only in the early 1920s; the old-stock liberal immigration policies, in Grant's view, were tantamount to "suicidal ethics which are exterminating his own race." He took issue with Franz Boas and others who emphasized the influence of environment and the potential for changes; what the melting pot (a biological, not a cultural, contrivance) really

accomplishes, Grant argued, is best exemplified by "the racial mixture which we call Mexican, and which is now engaged in demonstrating its incapacity for self-government."

Multiracial ancestry that is now presented to Americans as a variety of "white," was once held up as examples of the need for forced hypodescent to protect white racial "purity." As Grant states:

Whether we like to admit it or not, the result of the mixture of two races, in the long run, gives us a race reverting to the more ancient, generalized and lower type. The cross between a white man and an Indian is an Indian; the cross between a white man and a negro is a negro; the cross between a white man and a Hindu is a Hindu; and the cross between any of the three European races and a Jew is a Jew.

The great difference between most "black" and "white liberal" thinking today and Grant's overt racism, is that the former "whitens" all the crosses mentioned above except those between "Negro" and "white."

Jacobson reminds us that so salient are the differences among Nordics, Alpines, and Mediterraneans, that when Grant lumps them together at all, he does so only by the self-undermining phrase "so-called Caucasians." The term "Caucasian race" has ceased to have any meaning, he argued, except where it is used to contrast white populations with "Negroes," "Indians," or "Mongols."

The advocates of the new eugenics movement, such as Madison Grant and prominent eugenicist Harry Laughlin, worked hard to eliminate the old immigration law which opened America's doors to all "free white persons." Most of these so-called "whites" were not all that "white,"—that is, they were not of the ideal "Nordic" stock that Grant, Laughlin and their ideological confederates considered the truly "superior race" and the genetic base of the American republic. Jacobson summarizes the successful political activism that Grant, Laughlin and their comrades in the eugenics movement engaged in to protect the U.S. from "inferior races":

Their activism finally achieved success in 1924's Johnson Act - a quota system based on 2 percent of each group's population ac-

cording to the 1890 census. This formula was originally part of
the Report of the Eugenics Committee of the United States
Committee on Selective Immigration. That committee, chaired by
none other than Madison Grant and including Congressman Albert Johnson of Washington (the president of the Eugenic Research Association, 1923-1924), argued that a formula based on
the 1890 census rather than a more recent one "would change the
character of immigration of the stock which originally settled this
country." North and Western Europeans, read the report, were of
"higher intelligence" and hence provided "the best material for
American citizenship." Although the authors of the report alleged
that this was not a question of "superior" and "inferior" races, but
merely a matter of admitting an "adaptable, helpful and homoge-
neous element in our American national life," they did venture
that their formula would "greatly reduce the number of immigrants of the lower grades of intelligence, and of immigrants who
are making excessive contributions to our feeble- minded, insane,
criminal, and other socially inadequate classes." Citing data from
Yerkes's Army Intelligence Tests, the authors now poured very
old wine into the new bottle of eugenics: "Had mental tests been
in operation, and had the "inferior" and "very inferior" immigrants been refused admission to the United States, over six million aliens now living in this country, free to vote, and to become
the fathers and mothers of future Americans, would never have
been admitted."

The words "six million" have special significance,
since this racist immigration law would cost countless European Jews their lives during the 1930s and 1940s. They could
not be admitted, because, although officially "white" under
America law, they were among the "inferior races" the eugenics activists intended to exclude.

The Johnson Act did not invent the hierarchy of white
races. While the view of Madison Grant, Albert Johnson,
Harry Laughlin and their ilk seem extreme to us today, Jacobson reminds us that it is critical to recognize that figures far
more central to American political and intellectual life shared
many of their basic assumptions - Theodore Roosevelt, Calvin
Coolidge, Edward A. Ross, Frederick Jackson Turner, W.E.B.
Du Bois and Charlotte Perkins Gilman are among them. Herbert Hoover's Committee on Social Trends could enthusiasti-

cally laud the immigration act as selecting "a physical type which closely resembles the prevailing stock in our country." Authors such as Jack London, Frank Norris, Charles Chesnutt, James Weldon Johnson, John R. Dos Passos and many others accepted the idea of a hierarchy of "white" races.

Creating Caucasians or Finding Allies Against the Rising Tide of Color

Between the 1920s and the 1960s concerns of "the major divisions" would so overwhelm the national consciousness that the "minor divisions," which had so preoccupied Americans during the period of massive European immigration, would lose their salience in American culture and disappear altogether as racially based differences. Indeed, between the mid-1920s and the end of World War II, "Caucasian" as a "natural" division of humanity became part of a popular national catechism. Scientists "apply" the term "race" only to the broadest subdivisions of mankind, Negro, Caucasian, Mongolian, Malayan, and Australian," explained a 1939 handbook for high school teachers. "ALL THESE SCIENTISTS AGREE THAT NO NATION CAN BE CALLED A RACE," the text emphasized, self-consciously undoing the notions of "Aryan" and "Semitic" integrity.

Jacobson believes that the massive migrations of African Americans from the rural South to the urban North and West between the 1910s and the 1940s produced an entirely new racial alchemy in those sections. Mid-century civil rights agitation on the part of African Americans - and particularly the protests against segregation in the military and discrimination in the defense industries around World War II - nationalized Jim Crow as the racial issue of American political discourse. Both the progressive and the regressive coalitions that formed around questions of segregation and desegregation solidified whiteness as a monolith of privilege; racial differences within the white community lost their salience as they lost their reference to important power arrangements of the day. And, finally, events in Nazi Germany, too, exerted a powerful influence on public opinion.

Jim Crow whitened people who would not otherwise have been "white." When four dusky Armenians petitioned in court for "white" status after a lower Massachusetts court found them to be "Asiatic" and thus ineligible for citizenship, the Circuit Court judge *In Re Halladjian* (1909) ruled in their favor by citing Southern segregation statutes that placed Armenians on the "white" side of the line. They were suspiciously dark, but claimed no relationship to the despised "Negro."

Increased uprisings and demands for independence in Europe's African, Caribbean and Asian colonies, as well as the rise of non-white nations such as Japan and China, impressed upon many "white" elites the need for a reconstruction of the "white race." In other words, there were not enough "superior" Nordics to fight off all these "colored" peoples. More "white races" had to be invited into the "white" club with full membership. Lothrop Stoddard's *The Rising Tide of Color against White World Supremacy* (1920) and *Reforging America* (1927) sounded the call to "white" solidarity. There had to be some sense of shared destiny among Nordics, Alpines and even Mediterraneans if the "white race" was to survive the "white civil war" of World War I, the Bolshevik Revolution's challenge to European capitalism and civilization, and the insistent demands of colonized "colored" peoples for independence and equality. Note the similarity between this reasoning and colonial America's need to create a sense of European solidarity against slaves and Indians.

The treatment of race in the sciences underwent fundamental changes in the years between the eugenic triumph of 1924 and the post-World War II period. Social scientists such as Ashley Montagu, Ruth Benedict and Julian Huxley proclaimed "race" and "racial purity" to be myths. However, there was a double standard that is still inherent in American "racial" liberalism that Jacobson could have given more emphasis. Concepts such as the "Aryan race" or the idea that Jews, Mediterraneans, Germans, etc. constituted different races was denounced in forceful, moral terms. Students were told to NOT see those groups as "races." If they did, then their own moral blindness and intellectual stupidity were at fault. At the same time, they were told that the "purity" of the "white race" was false and that it was nonsensical to describe someone with a small amount of "black" ancestry as "Negro." However, scholars would simply blame "society" for those beliefs and encouraged their students to use those myths as if they were true. We still see their handiwork. If you accuse a "liberal" scholar of putting the "African American" label on any person he suspects of "black blood," regardless of how they saw themselves or how they were accepted within their own communities, he will smile condescendingly and say some version of, "Of course, I know better, but society..." However, if a student uses "Aryan" as a racial term or refers to Germans, Jews, Italians, etc. as "races," he will go to great pains to correct the student as an individual. If the student persists, social and academic censure will follow. In other words, academia takes responsibility for making sure that the "hierarchy of white races" does not resurface. In the case of forced hypodescent, however, they blame "society" and pretend to be helpless.

Jacobson shows that the most liberal scholars of "race relations" de-legitimized the old hierarchy of "white" races in order to replace it with the equally unscientific myth of "three great races" or "divisions of mankind" - the Caucasian, Negroid and Mongoloid" (sometimes adding the Australoid, or Australian aboriginal). They took pains to take their "knowledge" to elementary and high schools, instructing teachers throughout the nation to emphasize the idea of one unified "Caucasian" race when before there were Irish, Jewish, Slavic, etc. "races." Imagine what could happen if they took the same pains to denounce forced hypodescent and "white racial purity" with the same fervor they used to intellectually destroy the "Aryan race."

The intellectual reworking of "race" reached its zenith in *The Race Concept* (1950, 1952), a series of statements hammered out by the world scientific community under the auspices of the United Nations Educational, Scientific, and Cultural Organization (UNESCO). Again, it promoted contradictions. The human race is characterized by an "essential and undeniable unity," yet there are "three great races" (Caucasian, Negroid, and Mongoloid). Much of this work is devoted to attacking the doctrine of the "Aryan" race, especially the traditional belief that Jews are a "race." The method for doing this was to emphasis the "whiteness" of Jews and free them from the implied stigma of Asiatic or other non-white descent. The genocide suffered by European Jews was the moral foundation upon which the denunciation of the concept of Jews as "non-Aryan" or "non-white" was promoted as the moral responsibility of both institutions and individuals. Notice that, if you use the terms, "Jewish race," or "Aryan race," most people (especially if they're educated) will take individual responsibility for correcting you. They rarely feel such responsibility for correcting those who espouse the "one drop" myth—probably because the people who are the official arbiters of what is and is not "racist" ("black" and "white liberal" elites) support it.

Among the self-conscious popularizations of this new, post-Nazi racial economy of "difference" was a public exhibit entitled "Races of Mankind" based on Ruth Benedict's pamphlet of the same name. It was developed by the Cranbrook Institute of Science in 1943 and purchased by the American Missionary Association as a traveling show for use by any group "seeking to promote interracial understanding and goodwill through the medium of education." The main points of the exhibit were: 1) Nationalities are not races; (2) Jews are not a race; (3) There is no "Aryan" race; (4) the "Negro" is racially mixed (as opposed to that former "mongrel" the Mexican or other Hispanics); (5) There are three great "races" of mankind - white, black and yellow; (6) the "Caucasian" race has darker (West Asiatic) and lighter (European) branches. This was a conscious effort to expand the "white race" even further - to include Turks, Central Asians, Middle Eastern and North African peoples under the "Caucasian" umbrella. We still see this today in affirmative action forms that define "white" for us. The stigmatization of racial mixture as "Negro" is still with us. When many "white" mainstream newspapers editorialized against the "multiracial" census category, the repeated refrain was that all "blacks" are racially mixed (implying that "whites" are "pure" with Hispanics and their thoroughly mixed racial ancestry conveniently disappearing).

The Dawning Civil Rights Era: The Role of the Communist Party in Creating the White/Black Dyad

The American Communist Party, throughout the 20th century, was heavily involved in civil rights work. Indeed, only people on the far Left felt really free to openly advocate complete racial equality. However, the Communist Party, true to its Stalinist heritage, often undermined its own work by trying to make reality fit ideology.

The Sixth World Congress of the Comintern in 1928 adopted a "Black Belt Thesis" on "Negro national rights" that portrayed the problem of a despised caste as one of a "nation" with its own stable language, homeland and economic life similar to the national homelands that made up the Soviet Union. This was nonsense, of course, but the American Community Party used the fact that "Negroes" outnumbered "whites" within a "black belt" area of the South to invent the notion of a "Negro nation" with territorial rights and cultural consistency. The Communist Party did not concern itself with minor details such as the "ethnic cleansing" that would be involved in creating this "black nation" and the fact that many people claimed against their will by "Negroes" did not want to be part of any separate nation. This notion has also been embraced in various forms by Trotskyists, Maoists, etc. If you believe a people to be a "nation," then you are conceding authority to them over individuals within that "nation." The Communist Party legacy in American liberalism does seem to encourage the idea that a stigma (the "one drop" myth, for example) is really a valid or "national" identity. During the 1970s, this idea of a national "homeland" was extended to Chicanos in order to please the more militant activists.

As the Party pushed the fight against racial discrimination to the top of its political agenda, it also bullied its European-origin members to think of themselves simply as "white workers" - people with no separate "national" rights who suffered no discrimination except that common to the working class. There would be no Jews, Finns, Slavs, etc. but only a monolithic band of "white" workers "united" in struggle with their "Negro" counterparts. The Communist Party was the major influence on the Left in legitimizing the binary system of "race" in the U.S. Its definition of "nations" and "minorities" set "Negroes" on a plane of society far removed from any other group in American society.

Part of the Communist Party doctrine of a "Negro nation" was its insistence that other groups did not qualify as "nations" or "minorities" because they "are gradually being amalgamated with American people into the melting pot from which has emerged the American nation." I wish to add here that it is no wonder the Communist Party supported the "one drop" myth. To admit that the mixed-race or even "white" descendants of "Negroes" were NOT "Negro," would be a denial of its absurd definition of a "nation."

The White/Black Dyad Becomes the Central Tenet of Liberal Thought

Jacobson's view that the white/black dyad makes all peoples defined as neither "black" nor "white" invisible mirrors my own research, only I add multiracial to the groups he cites. While bigots like Senator John Rankin were railing against the "Kikes" who were trying to "mongrelize the nation," the weight of American culture was steadily and inexorably reducing the polity to a simple dyad of black and white—a scheme in which the former white races vanished into whiteness, and in which, so far as public discussion went, American Indians, Filipinos, Pacific Islanders, and Mexican and Asian immigrants and their children vanished altogether. By the civil rights era library shelves were filling up with books bearing titles like:

White and Black: Test of a Nation; *Crisis in Black and White*; *Confrontation: Black and White*; *Black Families in White America*; *Race Riots in Black and White*; *Black and White: A Study of U.S. Racial Attitudes Today*; *Black Children*,

White Dreams; *Beyond Black and White*; *Assertive Black, Puzzled White*; *Black and White Self Esteem*; and *White Justice, Black Experience*.

This deluge of books with black/white themes was sending a clear message: that Americans come in only two "races"—"white" and "black." Who are those people who don't look white or black? Must be foreigners. It is no wonder that Hispanics and Asian-Americans constantly complain about being assaulted with questions such as "What country are you from?" or "Do you speak English?" Native Anglo multiracials are puzzled as to why they are often assumed to be "foreign." The answer is clear. Pick up any newspaper and see articles with phrases such as "all Americans, both white and black," or "Americans of both races." If you're sick of being a "foreigner," end the black/white dichotomy!

Jacobson gives credit to Carey McWilliams, an architect of the "nation of nations" tradition in American social thought, for his refusal to lose sight of the overall complexity of the American mosaic and for his refusal to make "race" identical with "the Negro" in American political life. Unlike Gunnar Myrdal and other social scientists, who would effectively expel from consideration those pegged neither as "white" nor as "black," McWilliams wrote about the plight of American Indians, Mexicans, Puerto Ricans, Filipinos, Japanese and Chinese in *Brothers Under the Skin* (1942). However, even McWilliams could not overcome the doctrine that "color" was the central division of American life:

> But even so, "color" and the "Color line" had become for McWilliams the primary organizer in thinking about American diversity. Indeed, if he carefully eschewed the simplicity of black-and-white, he did depict the political landscape in a binary of color/not color that consolidated whiteness itself.

After the Civil Rights movement opened up much of "white" society by securing laws against "racial" discrimination, some of the "forgotten" neither "white" nor "black" ethnic groups began to make themselves heard and couldn't be ignored—the various Latino and Asian groups as well as American Indians. The Left was therefore forced to change its cherish dyad of "white" versus "black" for one of "whites" versus "people of color." These terms all make about as much sense as "Aryan" and "non-Aryan."

Unfortunately the Left is still wedded to the white/black dichotomy. A new example is Noel Ignatiev's "New Abolitionist" movement and its journal *Race Traitor*. He dismisses the importance of "other races" and views "whites" as a monolithic army against "blacks," from whose ranks some "whites" will gallantly defect and turn "traitor." His views are similar to those of the far Right in that he believes that "race treason" is possible. Like too many leftists, he tries to put a "positive" spin on a racist concept.

Conclusion

When you read Jacobson's history, you can see why liberals and leftists tended to oppose the Multiracial Movement. Without monolithic "blackness," there can be no monolithic "whiteness." If the movement succeeds, "white" liberals and leftists become less "white." Ethnic "minorities" such as Latinos, Arabs, etc. also stand to lose some of the "whiteness" they have claimed via their unacknowledged interracial ancestry.

We must be aware of the history of this "racial alchemy" and not hesitate to use it to fight the liberal and left-wing devotion to "white purity" and hypodescent. Even more so, we must be cognizant of the fact that "racial" categories have never arisen from some common will of the people, but from the machinations of elites who seek to divide the population in ways that serve their own political and economic needs. They have both created and eliminated "races" according to THEIR needs, not ours. We must also take advantage of what freedom is left in this country and remember that we are still citizens with the right to speak out, not helpless victims of hypodescent. The knowledge and research provided by scholars such as Matthew Frye Jacobson, Lawrence R. Tenzer and others are ideological weapons in our hands. Will we have the courage to use them?

XI. National Public Radio Promotes the "One Drop" Myth
Originally published in *Interracial Voice* at
<http://www.interracialvoice.com/powell13.html>

On May 15, 2001, I heard Juan Williams on "Talk of the Nation" and "black" journalist and professor Neil Henry (author of *Pearl's Secret: A Black Man's Search for his White Family*) tell their audience of millions that "one drop of black blood makes you black." They said this as a FACT. The Latinos, of course, were conveniently not mentioned. If the "one drop" myth were true, then nearly all Latinos would be "black." That's why Latinos are now spoken of as a separate "race" (while leaving the escape hatch that Latinos can be "of any race"). Somewhere a person of mixed ancestry who is struggling with whether or not to reject hypodescent listened to Juan Williams and was persuaded that he has "no choice." Somewhere some "whites" who are confused about why some people call themselves "black" when they don't have that phenotype have learned from "the experts" that a good non-racist liberal defines "black" by "blood drops."

On May 17, NPR continued its promotion of forced hypodescent by interviewing Earl Lewis and Heidi Ardizzone, the supposedly "black" and "white" authors, respectively of *Love on Trial: An American Scandal in Black and White.* Their book is a history of the infamous 1920's "Rhinelander" case, in which a high society poor excuse for a man named Leonard Rhinelander tried to get his marriage to quadroon Alice Jones annulled because she allegedly "lied" about her "race."

Lewis and Ardizzone, like Neil Henry, are advocates of the idea that anyone who even might have a "drop" of the dreaded "black blood" is instantly a member of the "black race" and "African American" ethnic group. They want people to believe that you can be "black" without even knowing it. Non-black phenotypes and cultures are dismissed as unimportant. Note again that, through silence, they pay tribute to the greatest "passers" of all, the Latinos and Arab-Americans, by being careful not to mention their embarrassing relationship to the "race" they claim to champion.

Ironically, the books cited above lead one to question most of the "mulatto elite" values their authors hold dear. Neil Henry claims that his quadroon great-grandmother, Pearl was "proud" to be "black." However, her life story tells of a woman who "walked" the color line, even in Jim Crow St. Louis. Pearl took "white" lovers and did not behave the way a "respectable" light-skinned credit to the "Negro race" was supposed to behave. Pearl's "secret" was that she kept in touch with her "pure" white family in Louisiana after moving to St. Louis. She was afraid to tell her "Negro" family about it because she feared ridicule. As every good, black-identified "mulatto elite" person knows, "white" genes are to be cherished as a source of beauty, intelligence and "good" hair, but "white" people are to be rejected as "the enemy."

Neil Henry tells of a trip he took to Greece in which Greeks started speaking to him in their native tongue because he "looked Greek" to them. Neil relates this tale with typical "mulatto elite" astonishment at being assigned a "superior" identity. He can't get over it. Henry's family is nearly all "mulatto elite" or mixed to varying degrees, with typical "mulatto elite" values. Young Neil must be the best student in school in order to prove to "whites" that "blacks" aren't inferior. He must be "proud" of his [black] "race," while cherishing light skin and "good" hair. He must consider himself indisputably "black" even though he seems to have nothing in common with the "real" black kids. His culture is too "white" for them. He denies the contradictions of his "black" public identity and his mixed-race reality.

In *Love on Trial*, Lewis and Ardizzone use their editorial prerogative to continually describe Alice Jones as "black" and "African American" as if these were objective facts. Yet, Alice was the daughter of immigrants from England. She had no ancestors among American "Negroes" or even mulattoes. Her mother was described as "pure white" and her father's ancestry was actually unknown. He was the son of a working class white Englishwoman and a father who was presumed to be from one of the colonies of the British Empire. To this day, Alice's paternal grandfather has not been identified—racially or otherwise. Her father, George Jones, was darker than "white" but otherwise had no Negroid characteristics. Culturally, the Jones family (including two other daughters) did not consider themselves "black" or "Negro" and did not participate in "Negro" organizations. Like many mixed families, they varied their answers when completing the "race" question on official documents. Sometimes they were "colored" and sometimes "white." The authors admit that "colored" was not synonymous with "black" or "Negro," and the Jones family did not consider an admission of "colored blood" to be synonymous with accepting membership in the "Negro race."

The irony, again, is that the actual facts of the case show the ambiguity of mixed-race status. If Alice had been "black," she would not have defeated Rhinelander's suit. She would not have acquired massive sympathy from working class "whites" as a poor working class girl mistreated by a cowardly, high society cad who professed his undying love and them submitted to the authority of his aristocratic father. Also, contrary to the "passing" myth (upon which the "lying" about "race" accusation rested), Leonard was well acquainted with Alice's parents, her sisters, and even a really "black" brother-in-law. He often visited their home while he was courting Alice. The jury realized that Alice's husband didn't care about her ancestry until his father put the screws to him.

Finally, it must be noted that Neil Henry (professor of journalism at the University of California, Berkeley), Earl Lewis (professor of history and dean of graduate studies at the University of Michigan, Ann Arbor) and Heidi Ardizzone (teaches American studies at the University of Notre Dame) are gatekeepers of official knowledge on "race." They KNOW that, legally, the "one drop rule" has no status or power. They KNOW that the "black" ancestry of their Latino, North African and Arab colleagues proves that. And yet they have jobs where they can spend all their time promoting the "one drop" myth at the taxpayers' expense.

Heidi Ardizzone says she's working on a second book called *Red Blooded Americans: Race, Mulattoes, and National Identity*. We've seen the propaganda we can expect from her. I suggest that she read my review of *Whiteness of a Different Color: European Immigrants and the Alchemy of Race*. Italian-Americans were once almost mulatto.

The real facts about "race" will never be taught at Berkeley or Ann Arbor. You will never hear the truth about "race" on National Public Radio. "Black" elites and their "white liberal" allies will see to that.

XII. Pissing on the Graves of Heroes
Originally published in *Interracial Voice* at
<http://www.interracialvoice.com/powell14.html>

(With the US now at war, this protest is especially appropriate.)

Everyone agrees that Calvin Clark Davis of Bear Lake, Michigan was an American hero of World War II. Everyone agrees he deserves to be posthumously honored for his service in helping our nation defeat the murderous, racist tyrannies of the Third Reich and Imperial Japan with The Purple Heart, World War II Victory Medal, European-African-Middle Eastern Campaign Medal, Good Conduct Medal, American Defense Service Medal, Air Medal, and Distinguished Flying Cross. Everyone agrees that the heroic Davis joined the Army Air Force, completing 50 missions against the Japanese. Transferring to Europe at his own request, Davis became a radio operator aboard a B-17 bomber. He died Nov. 30, 1944, along with other members of his crew, while attacking the oil refineries in Merseburg, Germany.

However, his country has chosen to "honor" him by pissing on his grave, labeling him with racist descriptions comparable to the Third Reich's terminology of "non-Aryan" and "untermensch."

The war hero Calvin Clark Davis, we are told:

- "passed for white." (*Traverse City Record-Eagle*)
- He had to "lie about who he was." (*Traverse City Record-Eagle*)

- He "claimed to be white." (*Traverse City Record-Eagle*, *Chimes*, student newspaper of Calvin College, Grand Rapids, MI)

- He "pretended to be white" (*BBC News*, *Associated Press*, *Los Angeles Times*, *The Holland Sentinel*)

- He "concealed his race" (Rep. Peter Hoekstra, R-Holland, MI)

- He was a "light-skinned black man" (Rep. Peter Hoekstra, R-Holland, MI, *Chimes*, *BBC News*, *Associated Press*, *Los Angeles Times*)

- He was one of the "blacks who passed themselves off as white" (*Chimes*, *Associated Press*, *Los Angeles Times*)

- He "faked being white" (*Associated Press*, *Los Angeles Times*)

- He was a "black man who pretended to be white" (*The Holland Sentinel*)

- He was a "light-skinned black" (*The Holland Sentinel*)

- He was "African-American" (*Traverse City Record Eagle*)

- He was a "'white' black airman" (*BBC News*)

We can thank the *Traverse City Record-Eagle* (Michigan) for at least using the term "multi-racial" to describe Davis instead of the odious, disgusting racist oxymoron, "light-skinned black." The multiracial movement is making some progress. Unfortunately, the news sources quoted above almost seem to be in competition as to who can insult Davis (and, by inference, all other multiracial whites) more.

As usual, before we blame "white" racists or "black" ones, the fault for initiating this racist travesty lies with a multiracial person who is devoted to the myth that any amount of "black blood" makes even a predominately European-descended person too inferior for the supposed honor of his own ancestry. Calvin Murphy, a cousin of Davis who never met the man, lobbied U.S. Rep. Pete Hoekstra, R-Holland and Rep. John Conyers, D-Detroit, to posthumously "honor" Davis by awarding the medals he earned to surviving family members. However, the "honor" is forever tainted by linking it with a racist description of Davis as "black"—a description he rejected during his lifetime.

The medals were awarded during a "Black History Month" celebration for a man who was not black. Several hundred students attended to be indoctrinated into the mysteries of the "one drop" myth and the implied inferiority of white persons with "black blood." Rep. Peter Hoekstra thinks that Davis made a "very difficult personal sacrifice" in order to serve his country. No, Rep. Hoekstra isn't talking about Davis' combat service or his death in battle. He claims that identifying as "white" was somehow a "very difficult personal sacrifice." Of course, in Rep. Hoekstra's eyes, this is only a "sacrifice" for persons tainted with the stigma of partial "black" ancestry (without the "escape hatch" of Hispanic or Arab ethnicity to protect you, of course).

Like the late New York Times book critic and author, Anatole Broyard, Davis was "blackened" after his death. Davis' case is also comparable to that of another military hero, Captain Michael Healy of the United States Revenue Cutter Service (now the U.S. Coast Guard), a white multiracial Irish-American who was proclaimed an "African American" and "black" decades after his death so "blacks" could claim a hero. Reared in the rural northeastern Michigan village of Bear Lake, Davis was a man of predominately European ancestry living among other European-Americans. He was not treated differently from anyone else. Is it so surprising then, that Davis would identify as "white"? He sure wasn't black or Negro. Just as in Broyard's case, ignorant fools claim multiracial whites who identify with their European heritage are passing, lying, pretending, concealing, faking their "true race." They even try to claim that the victim never considered himself white when all the evidence points in the opposite direction. This is somewhat like saying that a movie star really loves you only she has to hide it from her fans. When an individual does that, everyone agrees he needs professional help. When it's done in the name of the "black race," such delusions are presented as both real and noble. You can be sure that the people choosing to "honor" Davis as "black" wouldn't dare to "insult" a Hispanic or Arab with that word, even if the latter showed buckets rather than undetectable drops of the supposedly super-dominant "black blood." For some of us, there seems to be no honor in being too American.

In order to please alleged blacks and honor the "one drop" myth of hypodescent so dear to American blacks, Davis has been racially kidnapped and raped—posthumously—in the name of being "honored." Would any of the people who have so "honored" him dare to "honor" a Jewish-American war hero as a brave "non-Aryan" whose deeds proved the equality of "Aryans" and "non-Aryans"? Of course not! Jewish-Americans are smart enough to recognize the insult in using that racist terminology—no matter how sugar-coated. Honor Calvin Clark Davis the war hero, but don't piss on his grave by labeling him "black."

URLs to some sample stories:

- http://www.record-eagle.com/2002/feb/022302.htm – War hero Cal Davis still serves his country.

- http://www.house.gov/hoekstra/21502.html – World War II hero concealed race to fight.

- http://www-stu.calvin.edu/chimes/2002.02.22/cmm4.html – Soldier honored for heroism, defying racial boundaries.

- http://news.bbc.co.uk/1/hi/world/americas/1828687.stm – "White" black airman receives military honour.

- http://www.hollandsentinel.com/stories/021902/new_021902038.shtml – Black man who pretended to be white gets posthumous honors.

Index

Backintyme Booklets

To order booklets using a credit card, either visit our web site or telephone. Booksellers should phone for terms and discounts. Any item can be returned at any time for full money back.

Backintyme
30 Medford Drive
Palm Coast FL 32137-2504
386-446-4909
www.backintyme.com

Antebellum Race Relations

America's Odd Two-Caste System: *Paths Not Taken, Part 1* – A

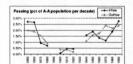

puzzle of U.S. history is the permanence of America's Black ethnic group. It is unique in two ways. First, others quickly blended into the U.S. melting pot, while African-Americans show no sign of assimilating after four centuries. Second, dozens of nations in both hemispheres imported millions of African slaves. Yet all but one absorbed their former slaves by intermarriage soon after freeing them. This book shows how both U.S. intermarriage and passing rose and fell over the centuries. $2.99, 32 pages, ISBN: 0-939479-11-7.

The Virginia Origin of the Two-Caste System: *Paths Not Taken,*

Part 2 – Four times in history, Americans absorbed people of biracial heritage. Each time, family members seen as Black were torn from those seen as White. Each time marked a path not taken, a time when history might have turned out differently. This book shows the origin of the two-caste system in 1676 Virginia. $4.95, 40 pages, ISBN: 0-939479-12-5.

The Destruction of the Louisiana Creoles: *Paths Not Taken, Part 3* – The United States absorbed populations of mixed Afro-European heritage by splitting them into White and Black branches on four occasions. Tells about the Louisiana Creoles from 1803 to Reconstruction. This book examines what happened the first time that Americans acquired territory already inhabited by an established biracial culture. $2.99, 20 pages, ISBN: 0-939479-13-3.

The Invasion of Spanish Florida: *Paths Not Taken, Part 4* – After

wresting Florida from Spain in 1821, the United States imposed its own customs. The most traumatic was the segregation of Whites from Blacks, even within families or among the elite. By 1840, the last few biracial families had emigrated to other former Spanish colonies, split into White and Black branches, or fled to Maroon communities in the wilderness or the Bahamas. Six biracial families exemplify how Spanish Floridians responded to the cataclysm: Edimboro, Sanchez, Pacheco, Kingsley, Hernandez, and Levy. All six families were deeply involved with slavery as slaves, masters, or both. This is their story. $3.95, 32 pages, ISBN: 0-939479-14-1.

The De-Assimilation of South Carolina: *Paths Not Taken, Part 5*

– Confederate law disallowed Negro combat soldiers. Hence, most historians agree that negligibly few Negroes joined the Confederate Army and fought to preserve slavery. Yet a few insist that hundreds of African-Americans did precisely that. Both are correct. The semantic trick is that the terms *Negro* and *African-American* denoted different things in 1860s South Carolina. This book tells about the tragedy of the South Carolina elite. They were wealthy biracial landowners, who were legally White in 1850, but found themselves re-labeled Black when the color line suddenly shifted in 1895. $2.99, 16 pages, ISBN: 0-939479-15-X.

Civil War History

America's Palatka Adventure: War Service of a Racing Yacht –
The world's most famous sailboat, who gave her name to the America's Cup Regatta, became a Confederate blockade-runner in the war. She was sunk in Dunn's Creek, near Palatka, then refloated to become a Union blockader. This is her story. $4.95, 40 pages, ISBN: 0-939479-19-2.

Yulee's Railroad – The story of Florida's first railroad, and of the men who built and ran it. For four years, the Union held both ends; the Confederates held the middle. Olustee was fought over it. Rosewood's survivors owed their lives to it. $3.95, 28 pages, ISBN: 0-939479-18-4.

A History of The Minstrel Show – Minstrelsy was a unique American art that began about 1840, peaked around 1860, and continued as the most popular theater in America until about 1895. Examines the minstrel show's folk origins, outlines a typical performance, and traces its legacy in American entertainment today. $3.95, 36 pages, ISBN: 0-939479-21-4.

The Evolution of Rifle Tactics – "Why didn't soldiers take cover?" Answers a question often asked of living history interpreters. Explains why it took 65 years for tactics to catch up with Claude Minie's invention of the military rifle. $5.95, 52 pages, ISBN: 0-939479-16-8.

The Evolution of Indirect Fire – "Why didn't cannons shoot from behind a hill?" Sequel to *The Evolution of Rifle Tactics*. Explains why cannons deployed in the front line to fire directly at the enemy, until inventions from around 1890 changed artillery tactics. $4.95, 48 pages, ISBN: 0-939479-20-6.

The Longstreet Controversy – Between 1872 and 1890, Confederate General James Longstreet's reputation was destroyed by two falsehoods: that Lee's defeat at Gettysburg made the South lose the war, and that Longstreet caused Lee's defeat. The first was the unplanned consequence of public enthusiasm for the site. The second was character assassination by Jubal Early. $3.95, 28 pages, ISBN: 0-939479-17-6.